SECOND TO NONE

The Biography
of
Khun Yay Maharatana Upasika
Chandra Khon·nok·yoong

DHAMMAKĀYA FOUNDATION
PATUM THANI, THAILAND

from the same distributors

Academic
9789748920931   Buddhism into the Year 2000
9789748235875   Palitext CDROM Database of the Entire Pali Canon

Biography
9789748940946   The Life & Times of Luang Phaw Wat Paknam
9789749274668   Second to None: Khun Yay Chandra Khon·nok·yoong

Childrens'
9789748237954   Lion & a Woodpecker
9789748237985   The Malicious Fox
9789748237961   Matuposaka Jataka
9789749162033   Buddha's Life
9789745195264   Values Education for Peace: Peace Ethics for Kids
9789744990914   Values Education for Peace: Peace Ethics for Youth
9789746435932   The Lord Buddha's History

Scripture-Based Exegesis
9789749058732   Buddha's First Teaching
9789749095218   Vanijja Sutta
9789749058718   Fruits of True Monkhood
9789749099612   Reforming Society means Reforming Human Nature
9789748277707   Man's Personal Transformation
9789749313558   Manual of Peace
9789749423035   Visudhivaca Vol.1
9789743498152   Visudhivaca Vol.2
9789748761824   Blueprint for a Global Being

Lifestyle, Meditation, Inspirational
9789749498415   Living in Peace without Worry
9789748785547   Start Meditation Today!
9789749360781   How to raise the children to be Good People
9789740938002   Pages to Happiness
9789810577575   Tomorrow the world will change
9789749498408   Right Understanding (Optimistic Wisdom)
9789740973768   Warm Hearted Family
9789749478301   Pearls of Inner Wisdom (pocket)
9789810585211   Pearls of Inner Wisdom
9789810596378   Journey to Joy
9789810800444   Lovely Love
9789745193109   Family Day by Day

Foreign Language
9789749180914   De levensgeschiedenis van Luang Pou Wat Paknam (NL)
9782953405615   La vie et l'oeuvre de Luang Pou Wat Paknam (FR)

Instructional
9789749229330   The Ordination
9789749455371   Little Book of Buddhist Chanting
9786167200071   Little Book of Buddhist Chanting (London Edition)

Commemorative
9789749297414   Sharing is Great: Tsunami

2

This book is dedicated to Kuhn Yay
Maha Ratana Upasika Chandra Kohn·nok·yoong
through whose example we can
appreciate the profundity of the Dhammakaya Tradition
down to the present day.

A Dhammakaya Foundation paperback
First edition 2005
Second revised edition 2010

Published by the Dhammakaya Foundation
Department of International Relations
Khlong Luang, Patumthani 12120
Thailand

National Library of Thailand Cataloging in Publication Data

Dhammakaya Foundation.
Second to None: The Biography of Khun Yay Maharatana
    Upasika Chandra Khon-nok-yoong
Bangkok: Dhammakaya Foundation, 2005.
174p.
1. Khun Yay Maharatana Upasika Chandra Khon-nok-yoong (1909-2000)
I. Title
294.30922

ISBN 974 92746 6 0

Printed and bound in Thailand by
SMK Printing Co. Ltd., 5/1 Soi Wannawan 2, 14 Charoen Nakorn Road, Klong
Klongsarn, Bangkok 10600. Tel. +66-2-4389972 to 3, 8620133 to 4. Fax +66-2-439
smkprinting@smkprinting.com

Contents

Contents

1
Prologue

Most people's lives are preoccupied only with the pleasures of the senses, spending all day thinking about the temptations of eating, sensuality and power. When one's intentions are impure, it leads one's speech and actions to be impure making one selfish and a puppet to one's emotions.

The way of life of a person willing to 'swim against the tide' of the mundane and the profane is a demanding one. It demands practice rather than chatter and a mind filled with merit and goodness — the marks of a person who keeps up meditation practice throughout their life. It can demand a life of perfect celibacy — the sort of life looked up to even amongst the community of Buddhist monks. It is hard to find a person of such pure intentions anywhere in the world — and the chances of finding such a person diminish with the passing years and the current swing of society towards material values.

One such person, however once walked the Earth in the form of a Buddhist nun called Khun Yay (Maha Ratana Upasika Chandra Khon-nok-yoong), the founder of Wat Phra Dhammakåya which is one of the biggest Buddhist temples in Thailand. 'Khun Yay' is a title meaning 'respected lady master of advancing years' — a name she was referred to by her closest disciples.

This book is the story of her life — a woman whose every breath was filled with meritorious deeds, whose every mental moment was directed towards Nirvana — her main virtues being gratitude, respectfulness, cleanliness, discipline, compassion, perseverance and being a good friend to others.

Under the tutelage of The Great Abbot of Wat Paknam, Khun Yay devoted her life to studying the knowledge of *Dhammakāya*[1] – becoming as a result, someone who guided other peoples' lives towards spiritual wealth both in this world and the next, while elevating peoples' minds in the direction of Nirvana in the footsteps of the Buddhist saints. With others she shared something hard for most to give, which is inner virtue amassed through the self-training of many decades. She was more to her students than many of their own parents, giving them the spiritual dimension to their lives – linking the knowledge of *Dhammakāya* in the oral tradition from its founder down to the present day. The knowledge she transmitted is at the core of a community of millions of meditators throughout the world in the present day who are striving to perfect and bring peace to the world through meditation. Khun Yay once said, "Although I'm single, I have fledglings all around the world." Indeed, her compassion and example reaches those of all walks of life, in keeping with her name 'Chandra,' (the moon) whose soft light enchants everyone's heart.

In Thai Society it is often hard for people to break

---

1. known in Thai as '*vijjā dhammakayā*', this tradition is based on wisdom gained by those practising insight meditation beyond the attainment of hte body of enlightenment. It can be equated with the Threefold Knowledge, Sixfold Superknowledge and Eightfold Supranormal knowledge of the Buddhist Scriptures.

out of the social context they have been born into — unless they are truly exceptional. It is only by associating with sages, or by doing exceptional amounts of goodness that upwards mobility be effected. Khun Yay had what it needed to make that transformation. Her wiry and aged appearance belied her might in conquering the defilements of the mind. Her illiteracy belied extraordinary spiritual wisdom. Her two wizened hands belied the majesty of the huge temple she created with them. Through her virtue, Khun Yay was like a beautiful lotus flower growing from roots embedded in worthless mud. Not being able to read or write was no bar to her mastering supreme knowledge — allowing her to teach even disciples much better educated than herself. Being a nun in Thailand is often not the most well-accepted occupations yet Khun Yay fulfilled her duties so completely that by the end of her life she was accepted by the monastic community throughout the world.

This biography of Khun Yay's extraordinary life is a testimony to the goodness we have experienced from her – and although this can in no way fully repay the debt of gratitude we have to her, it can go some way to inform the future generations who had no chance to meet her in person, of her life of virtue as an example to those yet to come.

2
The Fields
of Nakorn Chaisri

Socati puttehi puttimā
Gomiko gohi tatheva socati
Upadhīhi narassa socanā
Na hi so socati yo nirupadhīti

Those who have children will have sorrow
because of their children. Those who have oxen
will have sorrow because of their oxen. Such
attachments are the origin of peoples' sorrow.

Nandana Sutta (S.i.108)

It was daybreak in the paddy fields of 'turn of the century' Nakorn Chaisri. A group of young men clad in dried palm-leaf hats and the rag-tag, drab-coloured waistcloths that identified them as farmers, hastened down the beaten pathway that followed the top of the dyke dividing the paddy fields. Yesterday they had sped along the same track — but today they had got up a few minutes earlier. In an uncommon show of enthusiasm to reach the fields first, they turned the final corner onto a patch of the quilt of crops always kept completely free of weeds — a patch that always yielded more than that of the neighbours. "Not again!" came the disappointed cry from the youths — seeing the gaunt silhouette of a girl already bent double — face to the ground, back to the sky — plucking weeds from her crop. No matter how

11

early they arrived each morning — she was always there first.

For this young girl with a straight back and a quick pace, her every step was gentle and full of awareness. Even when sitting her back didn't rest against the chair. She was filled with energy, despite her wiry appearance. Her hands were the big hands of a worker not *petite* and elegant like some women. The skin of her face was taut and smooth. Her eyes sparkled reflecting the compassion and sincerity within her heart. They were the kind of eyes that cast a spell over everyone who met her.

They called her 'Chandra'[1] - the family's surname being 'Khonnokyoong'[2] - daughter of a family of moderate means. There was thirty-five rai[3] to the family name. She had been born in the early morning of Thursday 20 January 1909. It was a time when the monks were out on almsround - something that traditionally foretold she would have to work hard all her life. Her father was called Ploy and her mother Pan. She was the fifth-born daughter in a family of nine children. Her father came from a relatively poor family compared to that of her mother.

Chandra had no chance for a formal education, because in those days there was no state education. Like most of the girls of her era, it was more common to be occupied with home duties, instead of being allowed to go to school. Chandra tended both the home and the field – something which demanded great fortitude from her. As a character, Chandra was very sincere but demanding of little.

Before dawn she would get up at three or four o'clock in the morning, taking the buffalos out to graze

---

1. meaning 'the moon'   2. meaning 'Peacock feather'   3.14 acres

the pasture. Morning and afternoon were spent planting and weeding the paddies. At midday, estimated from the position of the overhead sun, she would take the meal out to those working in the fields. She and her friends would take the water buffalos for washing every evening before returning them to the corral. At harvest time she would work continuously from dawn to dusk. Her earnest was apparent to those farming on neighbouring plots. They were impressed by her diligence and respected her for it. She earned the reputation as the most diligent in the village.

She was popular with her friends — who and loved to play with her. She got along with them all because she never took sides with anyone. She played equally with all of them. They used to play the 'tide-up-tide-down' game jumping a skipping rope that was held either high or low. For a joke a friend said 'tide up', 'tide down' but pulled Chandra's ear up and down instead of the rope, hurting her – but on the whole her childhood was fun. She loved to swim too. She thought of swimming every time she saw a pond. These were the formative years for her character of bravery, nature, wit and unlimited freedom. She was cheerful, impulsive and lively. Her father used to say that among all of his children, Chandra was the most trouble.

A buffalo, Aen, and her dog, Kiaw, were amongst the animals Chandra considered her pets. She loved all of them equally. She took good care of them all and played with her buffalos that worked the rice field. As they got old, they lost their teeth and were unable to work. In some places they would slaughter such old cattle — but Chandra continued to feed them well with young grass every day until they died of natural causes.

The parents taught their children to be honest to themselves and to others, to be diligent and never to waste time. The farmer's life made Chandra used to hardship and endurance because she had to help her parents with work all day long. When she worked, she never showed signs of weariness and always persevered despite difficulties. Helping in such a way, the family's financial status in the community gradually improved. She was never indebted to anyone financially. Her lack of chance for education never decreased her wish to learn — she made a classroom of the vast paddy fields of her youth.

Chandra loved life amongst the open fields of Nakorn Chaisri. Surveying the sea of rice fields and the unruffled heads of rice that seemed to extend as far as the eye could see, she felt a special contentment as if something inside her was set free. In the morning, the huge crimson orb of the sun against the horizon looked close enough to touch. Like all children, she wondered where the sun had come from. Even though she saw the sun every day just like anyone else, but her thoughts concerning her surroundings went beyond those of others. She dared to think of reaching the sun. Little did she know at that time, that her dreams might be truer than she ever imagined... She began to realize from an early age that she didn't see the world like other people. She had no interest in dressing up in fine clothes or wearing perfume, like the other village girls of her age. She never wore the jewellery she had. She grew up, worked diligently and presented everything she earned to her mother. When young men attempted to court her, they tried to start a conversation about this or that. She simply replied, "I don't know." She wouldn't chide them because she knew they would just pick on her. She simply said, "I don't know," and paid them no attention. They would soon give up on her. She didn't even build up their hopes, remaining in complete control of the situation.

Chandra used to ask her father whether he wasn't afraid of the evil of killing animals on the farm. He would reply, "I only kill for food to support the family. I never sell the meat for a profit and I would always go to make merit at the temple on Buddhist holy days." He thought that doing good would somehow make up for the evil he had done.

Although the family's life was generally peaceful and harmonious, father *would* drink his ten *satang*'s[1] worth of liquor along with the other men every day. The children respected the way, unlike other drinkers, that he would generally never return home angry, cursing or of a mind to reprimand them.[2] If the parents cursed their children, it was doubly traumatic because the children were bound to accept their parents' word. Thus, Thai parents had a great responsibility to set a good example to their children. Chandra's father was good-natured when sober, but would pick arguments with the mother if drunk.

It was circumstances in this context of parental respect which awakened Chandra, at the age of twelve, to her spiritual vocation. It was about

___

1. about a half-bottle
2. In days gone by, out of filial piety, Thai children had to persevere no matter how their parents treated them. They believed the parents' word to be sacred, accepting it without any doubt as to its truth. The belief in the inevitability of rebirth and karma was also accepted without doubt.

seven in the evening. Father had drunk his usual measure of spirits and was lying, as was his habit, in a hammock slung beneath the house. Dulled by the drink, he mumbled incoherently, under his breath. Mother and the children were in the house. The mother had some words she kept up her sleeve to mock the father under just such circumstances, to bring him back to sobriety. She would comment, "the sparrow is scrounging in another bird's nest" just loud enough for him to hear.

In any other family, a comment like this wouldn't have mattered. However, on that fateful day, mother's comment didn't stop father's mumbling. She repeated it louder and this time the teasing touched on a sore spot in his inferiority complex. His feelings were stirred to anger like the snake with a scalded tail. He summoned the whole family to his presence and asked, "Kids! Am I *really* a sparrow scrounging in another bird's nest? Is this the way your mother insults me?" The children kept startled silence, but father demanded an answer to his question more and more loudly. At last Chandra couldn't stand the tension any longer. Not wanting her parents to argue and in order to protect her mother she said, "Father, that's not what mother meant!" Like petrol poured on a fire, father's anger turned on his children. "If none of you will admit to your mother's abuse, may you be born deaf for five-hundred lifetimes!" The curse struck fear into Chandra's heart. The parent's word was sacred. Parents should never curse their children. "I am the one responsible for his anger", she blamed herself, "I will surely be born deaf in my next life! What can I do? If I apologize to father now, he will only get angrier." She remembered the folk custom of apologizing to relatives on their deathbed and figured it would be better to save her apology until then.

Two years later, in 1921, father was weakened by old-age. For a further year, the children took turn in nursing him. On the morning of the last day of father's life, Chandra was spoon-feeding her sick father when suddenly he shuddered, his eyes rolling back in their sockets. Because she was young, she didn't know what it meant, so she just called her mother to look after him instead. When she arrived on the scene, Chandra went to eat something in the kitchen still oblivious and then took a boat, punting out into the fields alone to check the November crops according to her normal duties. However, something happened beyond her worst expectation. She returned to find the rest of the family weeping around her father's bed. All her brothers and sisters had had the chance to apologize to him . . . except her. She had missed her last chance.

Chandra didn't weep with them. She saw death as to be expected for all mortals. Life went on, but the fear of deafness in her next life lingered like a scar in her mind. "Now, where can I find father in order to offer my apologies?" she asked herself. She had no idea where to look and no friend she could turn to for this sort of advice. She sat down and resolved to recompense her debt — then she went to lay out father's corpse as was the tradition. Chandra prayed and implored father to come to her in her dreams, so she might have the chance to apologize to him . . . but he never came. Her elder cousin advised her instead to make as much merit as possible and transfer it for her father's benefit. He explained that if father were able to rejoice [*anumodāna*] in the merit she had made, she would be halfway forgiven.

Nevertheless, Chandra was dissatisfied with the advice. Though years passed by, the strength of the wish to find her father never diminished. She wanted to apologise 'in person' and felt the urgent need to find out where he had been reborn so she might speak to him there. She knew that good people go to heaven when they die and bad people to hell. "But where are heaven and hell? Where is he? And how can I find him?" — she had only questions but no answers. These were the thoughts that haunted her throughout her teenage years — so much so, that she had very little time to think of anything else.

In 1927 when Chandra was eighteen, she was overjoyed to hear news of the Great Abbot of Wat Paknam's discovery of the Dhammakāya meditation technique. She heard that the Wisdom of Dhammakāya arising from meditation includes knowledge of heaven and hell, such that the meditator can visit these realms for themselves. She felt like dropping everything and leaving for Wat Paknam that day — especially having seen the unsatisfactoriness of the household life from such an early age. However, leaving her home and her family was not as simple as that. Mother would stand in her way if she were to leave home to practise Dhamma. No-one would be able to understand why a young girl of her age should have such a strong vocation.

Chandra therefore waited another eight years until 1935 — when she was considered old enough to go and stay with her aunt in Bangkok and look for work. She turned over her share of the family land to her (ordained) younger brother and younger

18

sister. She gave away her jewellery and remaining wealth to others in her family. All she had left were the clothes she stood up in, a healthy body, a determined heart and a mission to seek out her father in his afterlife destination.

When she bowed at her mother's feet in farewell, telling her mother her intentions, her mother cried out in pity. She didn't want her daughter exposed to hardship and preferred that she just marry and settle down with a family like a normal person. She thought that Chandra would be happier if she stayed but Chandra knew that studying the Dhamma could not be postponed any longer. Some argued that one should save spirituality for one's old age, but Chandra saw that anything one did while young could come more quickly to fruition. Usually children must succumb to the power of their mother's tears but Chandra's determination was not so easily swayed — she had already made up her mind long ago to study the knowledge of *Dhammakāya* with the Great Abbot of Wat Paknam. Even though she loved and respected her mother, she made the distinction in her mind between what was comfortable for her mother and what she *had* to do in her quest for the Dhamma. She never let go of that gratitude to her mother, but at the same time didn't allow that to weaken her commitment to her mission to reach her father.

Mother eventually gave her two baht bus fare and although Chandra didn't really need it, accepted it anyway out of consideration for her mother's feelings. That was how she came to leave her home, not looking back, but single-mindedly intent to

do whatever necessary, to attain the path out of suffering. Even though she had no idea what obstacles
would stand in her way or even whether she would
die before fulfilling her goal, she kept walking. All
she knew was that she had no alternative to finding
her father.

3
Stepping Stone to the Temple

Pasannam eva seveyya appasannaṃ vivajjaye
Pasannaṃ payirupāseyya rahadaṃ vudakatthiko

All those wishing for happiness should associate only with those inspiring of faith, avoiding those who don't inspire faith, sitting close by those who are inspiring of faith.

Mahābodhi Jātaka J.v.233

Chandra was from the provinces and coming into Bangkok she knew no-one. It wasn't by any means easy to be accepted at Wat Paknam. For a stranger to join the temple community or even the congregation, normally required being introduced to the temple by someone senior already held in esteem by the temple. Chandra had no direct contacts. At first she stayed at the house of some relatives. Meanwhile she sought employ in a family who practised meditation at Wat Paknam. She waited for an opportunity to present itself.

Eventually the person she was looking for came in the guise of Khun Nai Liap Sikanchananand who was a lady of aristocratic stock who lived in Saphan Han. Khun Nai Liap was already well-known to the legendary abbot of Wat Paknam. She was considered a major patron of Wat Paknam, having brought the midday meal for the monks and novices there regularly for more than twenty years. Khun Nai Liap's family was an influential and wealthy one. They were landlords for many kilometres of shopfronts and had their own import-export business. Chandra saw that this family would be the connection she needed to introduce herself to Wat Paknam. After due consideration she decided to seek employment with this family and was accepted as a maid.

Although from a relatively well-to-do family herself, Chandra had to stoop to being a maidservant in order to give herself the chance to attain the Dhamma, her ultimate aim. For her part she saw the family as a stepping stone by which she could make her way to Wat Paknam as soon as possible. When Chandra started to work for Khun Nai Liap, although for her domestic service was only a means to end, nevertheless she showed her willingness in all her duties without considering them chores. She thought of her work as merely helping to keep her mistress's home in order and being a steward for that family's wealth.

By habit, Chandra was diligent anyway, with discipline and perseverance engrained in her character. She loved cleanliness. Her honesty shone forth to others, to the point that it was not long before she was loved and trusted by all in the household. She was promoted from maid to head of the domestic staff within the space of her first week. Khun Nai Liap felt reassured that any task delegated to Chandra would be fulfilled without disappointment. With Chandra at home, Khun Nai Liap could leave the house knowing it was in safe hands. She was so much in Khun Nai Liap's confidence that Chandra, rather than her own children, was the one to be entrusted with the key of the family strong-room, where all the family's cash and jewellery was kept! It was a room inside which only Khun Nai Liap herself and Chandra were allowed. Chandra was patient and in the long run, her opportunity to start her study of meditation came in the personage of the (then) lay-woman teacher Thongsuk Samdaengpan.

Upāsika Thongsuk was thirty-six when they met — nine years older than Chandra. She was burly in appearance and tough having survived a childhood of considerable hardship. According to the usual protocol, she had been accepted into the meditation workshop of Wat Paknam, which in those days was no easy matter. She had had to pass an inquisition by a senior already adept enough to meditate there. They had asked her questions impossible for the man in the street to answer — questions only those who had already attained the *Dhammakāya* would have any chance of answering. The questions ensured that those entering the meditation workshop had already steadfastly attained the *Dhammakāya*. The questions were not designed for people or even angels to answer but were fathomable by the inner body of enlightenment alone. Nevertheless, Khun Yay Thongsuk had been allowed to conduct meditation research because her meditation attainment was considerable.

The family invited this teacher from Wat Paknam because besides being able to conduct meditation research, the Great Abbot had entrusted her to *teach* meditation outside the temple. Chandra had intended from the start to practise meditation with the teacher and hearing the news that she would soon visit the household again, Chandra was filled with joy and expectation. She knew that Upāsika Thongsuk would be the one able to teach her the knowledge she needed, if anyone could. Chandra wanted to start meditating with the teacher immediately like the rest of Khun Nai Liap's family. At the same time she knew that in her present status as a mere maidservant, she could not take such a privilege for granted. Thus she looked for ways to serve Upāsika Thongsuk to bring herself to the teacher's notice as a worthy student. Only then might she be permitted to study meditation with the rest of the family. This meant that Chandra had to work even harder than before. Now she had to find time to make herself useful to the teacher. She made up the teacher's bed, dusted the mosquito net and laundered the teacher's clothes, ironing and folding them so neatly that they would be sure to capture the teacher's attention.

Several weeks later, as Upāsika Thongsuk was reflecting on her impeccable laundry, she asked Chandra "Do *you* want to try learning meditation sometime?" Hearing these words, Chandra felt exhilarated like a cat being offered the cream and replied to Upāsika Thongsuk, "There is *nothing* more in the world I would wish for – but I cannot just go upstairs and learn with the others in case my mistress objects." Upāsika Thongsuk thus obtained Khun Nai Liap's permission for Chandra to sit for meditation with the rest of the family.

The room upstairs where they meditated with Upāsika Thongsuk had been chosen because it opened onto the house's flat roof and was cool and free of mosquitos in the evening. Upāsika Thongsuk's usual way of explaining meditation was to have them focus their mind gently at the centre of the body, visualizing a crystal ball while repeating the mantra 'Sammā-Arahaṃ' silently to themselves. Even these simple instructions, at first seemed quite difficult to follow. Whenever Chandra closed her eyes and wanted to let go of the things of the world suddenly she found her mind filled with thoughts of work. She would peep at her mistress to make sure she wasn't thought to be neglecting her domestic duties. Sometimes it would be thoughts of the family she had left behind or images of the open fields of Nakorn Chaisri that bothered her. "Thought is the greatest hindrance to meditation," explained Upāsika Thongsuk with understanding.

Back at work, Chandra subsequently divided her time more strictly. She would try finish her chores more quickly each day so that she would have the time to sit for meditation alone. She had to sit in secret the most of the time out of consideration for her mistress who might otherwise accuse her of shirking. She slipped meditation into the gaps between her household chores. Nonetheless, it was hard for her mind to become unified when she had to look over her shoulder each time she sat for meditation. Her mind could not put aside the worry of being caught meditating. Even so, Chandra never diminished her perseverance and never complained. The concepts of boredom, disillusionment or despair seemed alien to her. Her urgent wish to find her father, kept her firmly persistent to train herself in meditation. She strove always in any task she set her mind to — with a joyous smile on her face that pre-empted victory. She was someone who never wasted any time and had no such thing as time free from doing good deeds.

When she closed her eyes to meditate, she did so in earnest, cultivating concentration at the centre of her body, determined to see the crystal ball for herself. Indeed, she meditated *too* seriously and it quickly brought on a headache and feelings of dizziness. She was determined to find the central point of balance of the mind. There were no remaining extraneous thoughts in her mind. She avoided the sort of effort that makes it uncomfortable to breath but her mind still did not reach a standstill. She could see nothing but darkness in meditation and this went on for weeks, without any glimpse of inner light.

Upāsika Thongsuk taught her always to keep her mind at peace with the visualisation and the mantra. She said:

> "Don't worry if you're not an overnight success. Don't use force on your mind. Don't squeeze your eyes shut. Don't be afraid of seeing nothing and if you do see something at the centre of your body, don't get elated or the newfound image will disappear again!"

Nodding in understanding, Chandra tried again to find a peaceful mind through meditation. She put aside her thoughts of success and temporarily shelved the wish to find her father. Sometimes she felt discouraged. It felt like she was running after a shadow. Sometimes she thought she was destined never to achieve inner experience[1] in meditation. Chandra would ask in desperation, "if there is Dhamma, why can't I see it for myself?" Upāsika Thongsuk, allowed Chandra to understand little by little that Dhamma certainly exists, but we need to work on ourselves to be able to recognise it. With practice, there will come a time when we have done the work needed to attain inner vision for ourselves.

Chandra continued to train herself in meditation. She focussed on bringing her mind to a standstill at the centre of her body, within the stomach, two fingerbreadths above the navel. At last, she received confirmation from Upāsika Thongsuk that her mind was beginning to become refined and began to understand that whether the mind wavers or not, one has to progress step by step. When the mind becomes sufficiently refined, it will reach a standstill of its own accord. Just like trying to catch a hen in a chicken coop, in meditation our mind needs to be undeviating in its aim. If we rush to catch the hen, it will fly away. Our efforts will be in vain. By contrast, if we call the hen gently, it will be befriended and easily caught. Similarly, it is impossible to control the mind by force. By slow and careful application of the mantra, irrespective of whether we can see the crystal ball clearly or not, in the end the mind will come to a standstill at its point of balance. It is only the coarse and foolish who habitually use force. Inner experience is a subtle thing and Dhamma study needs a light and buoyant mind. In meditation the mind needs to be maintained gently at the centre of

---

1. inner experience is the phenomenon experienced in meditation which depthens one's understanding of the reality of life and the world

the body — nothing more and nothing less — no preconceptions or anticipations. The centre of the body, gentle application of the mind and no thinking — no more knowledge than this is necessary to embark on successful meditation.

Chandra practised this step of the practice further, but one obstacle still remained. Images of home and family would pop into her mind and sometimes other visions she didn't want to see. Upāsika Thongsuk taught her to take no interest in her imagination:

"Let the mind take its natural course of transformation and always keep the concentration at the centre of the body. Maintain the concentration there with mindfulness. Entertain no other thought. Like the unwelcome visitor who comes to call, if we pay him no attention, he will soon leave of his own accord."

With persistence and a firm resolve, she applied subtle effort at the centre of her body whether the crystal ball was visible or not. Khun Yay resolved to spend her whole lifetime meditating, if that was what it needed to find her father. The weeks of practice turned to months and the months to years. The quest for success in meditation, entered into her very soul. At first she would just meditate in her free time but before long she would meditate while working too. Eventually, after two years, she was able to reduce the number of thoughts in her mind, leaving herself with a feeling of lightness and spaciousness inside. On one occasion she perceived a tiny pinpoint of light inside herself rather like a star in the sky.

Another night, Chandra sneaked up to the upstairs

room by herself. She was able to bring her mind to a 'standstill within the standstill' and her mind was able to penetrate through the centre going continually deeper on the central axis within. At first she saw a bright crystal ball firmly established at the centre of her body. It stayed with her even after her meditation was finished. She saw the image clearly whether her eyes were open or closed for two or three days. This she reported to Upāsika Thongsuk, who in turn taught, that looking at the very centre of the crystal ball, she would see herself. She did as she was instructed and could see herself brightly and clearly. The teacher told her to go through this form to the angelic body, into the Brahma body and the Formless Brahma body.[1] This she did and inside the Formless Brahma body she could perceive the *Dhammakāya* Gotrabhū[2] allowing her to attain the *Dhammakāya* right there in the upstairs room of her mistress's house. At this stage, the thought occurred to her that:

> "even though I see only a little Dhamma, I have never known happiness like this before. Not for my weight in gold would I give away this Dhamma I have known today. There is no other refuge for me anywhere, excepting this Dhamma I have attained."

Having attained the *Dhammakāya*, Chandra didn't rest but meditated further until her mind became yet more stable and bright. Having attained *Dhammakāya* Gotrabhū, Chandra remembered her father. She reported

1. Seeing oneself inside, the angelic body, the Brahma body and the formless Brahma body are successive stages of progress in the Dhammakāya technique.
2. The eternal interior existence of the human body which exists in the form of the Buddha, but with a crystal brightness more effulgent than a hundred, billion suns.

her progress to Upāsika Thongsuk while divulging her wish to help her father in his afterlife destination. She had no idea where to look for him, but even so Upāsika Thongsuk said that Chandra's wish was no great challenge. By attaining the *Dhammakāya* she had already done the hardest part.

4
Seas of Fire

Appamattā satimanto
Susīlā hoti bhikkhavo
Susamāhita saṅkappā
Sacittam anurakkhatha

Those who see the danger in the cycle of
existence should not be reckless, should have
mindfulness, have unblemished precepts,
Right Intention and cultivate the mind.

Mahāparinibbāna Sutta (D.ii.120)

Upāsika Thongsuk went on to teach Chandra how to harness the knowledge of *Dhammakāya* in order to seek for her late father, applying meditation to her task.

> "Keep the mind pure and refined. Bring the body of the *Dhammakāya* to superimpose on your own and make the determined resolution to meet your father."

She meditated for a long time until she knew that her inner experience was sufficiently refined to start the quest for her father. According to the methodology at that time[1], Chandra allowed her mind to disconnect from her physical body. Her mind became one and the same as the Buddha image inside which she had attained. The concern about where to find her father didn't worry her any more. Her mind was neutral, impartial.

---

1. As the meditation technique evolved in later years the mind no longer disconnected but went inwards through the centre.

The *Dhammakāya* inside would take her where she needed to go.

She felt her body crisped as she soared across the face of a sea of fire. The fire seemed to become less intense and was eventually reduced to smouldering. Her *Dhammakāya* was shining brightly as the surroundings[1] in which she found herself became more apparent. Around her, on all sides were living beings, haggard figures. Some were animals. Some were human. Some were human with the heads of animals. Some were animals with the heads of humans according to the individual retribution of the bad karma each had done during their previous lifetime in the human realm. All were having torment inflicted on them by the denizens[2] of hell. The instruments of torture differed from one being to the next. The denizens paused from their work in response to Chandra's presence. Using the *Dhammakāya*'s faculty for seeing and knowing[3] eventually she found her father, more emaciated than she remembered him and with no remaining strength. He had died here over and over again in the time since leaving the human realm from having had flame-engulfed, molten copper poured down his throat — instantly burning away all the flesh of his body, causing almost immediate death. Having died in such a way, he would almost immediately be reborn in the same predicament, the same thing happening over and over again until all his retribution be exhausted. He looked very sorry for himself. He was naked and

---

1. The fifth level of hell, Mahāroruva, where the victims' major retribution concerns having drunk liquor during their human lifetime.
2. Demons spontaneously arising in hell as a result of their victims previous karma which inflict retribution until the victim's karma is exhausted.
3. in Buddhism technically known as *ñāṇadassana*

his face was clouded like a man broken by sorrow. On seeing the *Dhammakāya* he didn't even have the strength to raise his hands in a gesture of prayer.

When he saw his daughter, he admitted to her, "I am suffering in hell because when I was alive I habitually drank liquor. I drank heavily – ten *satang* worth a day — a bottle for each day of my life. Not only that, I used to kill animals too. I often killed frogs, shellfish, crabs and fish. Sometimes I killed a chicken for a meal."

Only now did he realize these evils were too serious to be traded off against the good ones – that they were the sort of evil that stays with one even after death. "Now I am suffering to repay the price of my misdeeds. As I was dying, all the evil I had done during my life flashed before me." He had died with a clouded mind overcome by guilt. With tears running down his swollen face, he implored his daughter to help.

Chandra felt sorry for him and didn't want him to be exposed to the torments of hell anymore. She felt great compassion for her father, but had no idea how to help him. She felt like a non-swimmer, watching someone else drown. She was uncertain what to do. Upāsika Thongsuk sensed her hesitation.

"My father is trapped in hell because he used to drink, but I can't do anything to help!"

"Start by having your father request the Five Precepts[1] from the *Dhammakāya*," advised Upāsika Thongsuk. The *Dhammakāya* told father to follow the Precepts in its resonant voice. Once he had taken

1. The five rules of physical and verbal conduct which underpin human morality, namely refraining from killing, stealing, adultery, telling lies and drinking alcohol.

33

the Precepts Upāsika Thongsuk told Chandra to dedicate merit, making the wish that it reach her father.

Chandra made the resolution: "May the grace of the merit from having staked my life in meditation until attaining *Dhammakāya* be dedicated to assist my father break free of his torment."

The *Dhammakāya* instructed Chandra's father also to recall all the merit which he had made during his life. Father pictured the merit he had made. This merit, together with the Grace of the *Dhammakāya*, made his body light and drift upwards. As it happened, he had made quite a lot of merit in his life. His body started to change in appearance from emaciated to radiant. His body became swathed in angelic raiment. He started to drift upwards away from the hell realms, higher and higher, following Chandra's *Dhammakāya*. He drifted higher, entering the heaven realm until reaching Tāvatiṃsa — the 'Heaven of the Thirty-Three.'[1] He had his own heavenly mansion there, but his was neither bright nor beautiful like that of the other inhabitants. The *Dhammakāya* told him that his heavenly mansion was not bright because when he was alive, he had done a lot of evil things, as well as virtuous ones. He had drunk heavily and the merit of supporting his family had been sullied by killing animals to feed the hungry mouths of his children.

The *Dhammakāya* taught him to meditate using the mantra '*Sammā-Arahaṃ*' and his body began to look brighter than when he was in hell, developing a heavenly form appropriate to the Tāvatiṃsa heaven and he had a retinue of other angels which was of reasonable size. Seeing this, Chandra's sorrow from

1. The second lowest of the six heavens described in Buddhism.

34

the unfulfilled wish to find her father disappeared completely.

Finally she asked forgiveness for her childhood trespasses against her father, bringing her long-lived quest to completion. Father put his hands in a gesture of prayer and granted her forgiveness. He explained he had only cursed her on that occasion out of anger and in fact had no intention that his daughter be deaf – but if it were something still upsetting her, of course he granted his forgiveness. As they parted, Chandra reminded her father that he would have to keep up his meditation or else he would slip back into the hell realms from whence he had come.

Having fulfilled her quest, Chandra found she could see things clearly — according to reality. When we are born, we cannot escape old-age, sickness and eventually death. Through our physical existence alone we can gain nothing, because in the end, it all returns to dust. Our material wealth is like *borrowed* property. We cannot take it with us when we go. Through the Eye of the *Dhammakāya* she could see that when we die, we take with us nothing but the merit and the evil we have collected through our actions during our life — that we are born as a human being, the supreme opportunity in existence, with the aim in life to overcome suffering. The direct route to escaping suffering is by following the celibate life [*brahmacariyā*] and the highest merit of all is to ordain and keep the purest precepts. Most people think that it is only appropriate for old people to turn pious, but at the age of twenty-nine, Chandra was ready to renounce the lay-life. She wanted to go further with her meditation and conduct meditation research in the tradition of the Great Abbot of Wat Paknam. She worked even harder than usual for her mistress in order to earn extra consideration so that her mistress would find it hard to refuse if she were to ask the opportunity to go for a month's meditation retreat at Wat Paknam....

5
Newcomer at the Temple

Selo yathā ekaghano   vātena na samīrati
Evaṃ nindāpasaṃsāsu   na samiñjanti paṇḍitā

*Just as a mountain of solid rock remains unmoved by
the winds. The wise man remains unmoved by gossip
or flattery.*

Dh.23

It was about 1938 when eventually she made an
appointment with Upāsika Thongsuk to spend
a month of meditation at Wat Paknam. She was
willingly granted a month's leave by Khun Nai
Liap. Her mistress emphasized, "But after a
month, you will be coming back won't you?"
in response to which Chandra kept her silence.
Khun Nai Liap assumed for herself that Chandra
would surely be back at work one month from
then.

That night as Chandra slept, she dreamt that
she was standing on the bank of a wide river. A
ferry carried her across to the far side where she
saw a huge Bodhi tree covered in luxuriant green
leaves giving her refreshing shade from the heat
of the day. Once ashore she sat beneath the Bodhi
tree with the utmost of happiness . . . and it was
with this feeling that she awoke.

That afternoon, for the first time in her life,
Upāsika Thongsuk took her to Wat Paknam
Bhasicharoen to meet the Great Abbot. Clad in

saffron robes, he was a monk in his early fifties. His forehead showed determination, intelligence and uncommon strength of character. His glare was penetrating and yet compassionate — his presence resolute.

It was a typical Thursday afternoon at the temple. The Great Abbot was in the middle of giving a sermon on Dhamma practice at a pavilion near the kitchens. When Upāsika Thongsuk introduced Chandra to him, he raised his head and peered at her. After a brief silence he asked the rhetorical question, "What kept you so long?" Chandra didn't really understand what the abbot meant. She was only twenty-nine and young by comparison to most people in the temple congregation. She would have to look deeper to know the significance of his words – because it'd already been a long time that he'd awaited the person who was going to lead his team of meditators in research.

Without having to pass the usual examinations of mastery in Dhamma practice, the Great Abbot sent her straight into the meditation workshop. He allowed her to join the most highly experienced group of meditation researchers in the temple. When she first entered the meditation workshop it was like being in a foreign country because the people there spoke entirely of things she could not understand. They used technical terms and she could make no sense of anything they were talking about.

Even though she didn't fully understand why the Great Abbot had given her such special treatment, she wasn't complacent. She trained herself in meditation seriously, to try to be able to do meditation research like her seniors and to be able to serve the

Great Abbot to the full. The subtlety of her medita-tion gradually increased – more than she had ever achieved in the past. Inside her mind was brighter than a skyful of midday suns condensed into one.

As time passed by the Great Abbot started to challenge her with questions unfathomable by conceptual thought. The first question she re-ceived from him concerned checking the language of animals. One day when the Great Abbot was returning from the monastic refectory, he spotted two pigeons and challenged Chandra to find out the conversation that had taken place between them. He said that the two pigeons had been perched together on the temple roof. One pigeon had turned its head to face away from the other and then the two pigeons had flown off together in the same direction.

Without knowing any more than this, Chandra went away to meditate upon the *Dhammakāya*. She brought her mind deeper and deeper to a standstill at the centre, until when her mind was perfectly at a standstill, she was able to *understand* the pigeons and returned to the Great Abbot with the answer. The pair of pigeons had been husband and wife — the male had been asking the female about the route to their destination so that they would not get lost on the way. The female had turned her head away to recollect the route, before they both set off together in the agreed direction. The Great Abbot said only "Err! That's how it ought to be" in response to Chandra's answer.

From there he started to ask Chandra gradu-ally more and more challenging questions. Next morning he asked, "(Daughter) Chandra! This morning I was on my way back from the monastic refectory and I saw a person who was lame. Meditate to tell me if their astral body[1] was also lame!" Again Chandra was able to find the answer to his question. He never had a word of praise for anything done right. He would just say, "Err! That's how it ought to be" when the answer was correct and would say nothing if the answer was wrong.

The questions he asked got harder still. Even though Chandra had no education and had very little general knowledge of the world, yet she managed to obtain the right answers to the questions asked, because her faculty for 'seeing and knowing' was exceptionally precise. The others were never as precise as her because they didn't share her devotion to the meditation practice. Meditation research was her only goal and the only thing she thought about in life. All she wanted was to be able to keep up with the Great Abbot in his research. Khun Yay had to undergo extensive training before she could achieve mastery of her meditation. This applied particularly to the patience she had to exert in the face of gossip and discrimination.

When Chandra first went to live in the temple community, she received very poor treatment. As a newcomer she was low in the pecking order. She was also treated badly because she could not read or write and also because of the privilege afforded by the Great Abbot, of joining the workshop so quickly. In addition, she had come from an upcountry family background and people tended to ignore her because of this. It was up to her to adapt to her surroundings rather than *vice-versa* and this meant particularly her

---

1. The next inner body in from the physical, synonymous with the soul or spirit.

companions at the temple and the facilities. It was hard enough to further her studies in the meditation workshop without having to sort out problems in her personal life. However, no matter how badly she might be treated by her fellows at the temple, she took no interest, because the only thing she was interested in was meditating well enough to vanquish Māra.[1]

Nevertheless, the creature comforts provided to her by the temple were the *most* dilapidated and were only given to her because they had been *abandoned* by the others – whether it be her bed, chairs or mosquito net. At that time she didn't have anyone who she could turn to and no influence — so, she didn't let such mundane trivialities bog her down.

Normally the idea of a mosquito net is to protect against bites but the one she was given had holes in it so large that it offered no protection. Nonetheless, she received it with gratitude, thinking no more than to use it to ward off biting insects. She washed it clean and patched the holes herself.

The legs of the bed she was allocated were broken. The mattress stank and was infested with bedbugs. No thought of resentment crossed her mind, however, because she considered that the bed was merely to allow her sufficient rest to put her efforts into the practice of meditation. It was of no importance in itself. She was no carpenter, but repaired the bed as best she could, so that it was at least usable. She polished it so clean that it looked as good as new. At night when she was asleep on the mattress, the bedbugs emerged one by one and bit her, shocking

1. The personification of evil forces in the world which delude the unwitting into contentment with life in the cycle of existence. Can be escaped and defeated only by the practice of meditation.

her rudely awake each time. She hardly got a good night's sleep. Most people who slept fitfully as she seemed destined to do, would be irritable next morning and snap at others for anything untactful said — but that wouldn't have been Chandra. She found a small spittoon for herself and put it at the head of her bed. She put a white rag at the bottom of it and covered it with a scrap of paper. Each time a bedbug bit into her, she calmly picked it off and put it in the spittoon covering it with a fresh piece of paper. In the morning she released the bedbugs elsewhere. She relocated them one by one, until eventually, there were no more bedbugs left infesting her mattress. She was left with a clean and hygienic bed.

When it came to mealtimes the long-standing residents of the temple would never join her at the same table, because Chandra looked so thin and emaciated. They were suspicious of her long, straggly hair and sunken eyes. She was so thin that tendons stood out all over her body. They assumed that she was suffering from tuberculosis.[1] They didn't want to catch it so kept their distance. Even those serving up the food at the canteen, slung it abruptly into her chipped, enamel plate as if they were reluctant to give her food at all. Most people would be upset by such treatment – they might feel resentment, want to go home or run sobbing to the abbot — however Chandra was able to be a teacher to herself in this respect. She recalled that the reason she was there was to practise meditation, not to be cosseted. The only reason she had left home was to study the 'knowledge of *Dhammakāya*'. She considered each

---

1. Which was still deadly in those days and hard to cure.

meal to be a gift from the Great Abbot, gleaned from the faithful who wished the merit of supporting him as a field of merit.[1] It didn't matter how such food was served – there could be nothing wrong with such auspicious food, no matter how it was served up.

She saw everything in a positive light. If she was treated abruptly by the canteen staff, she assumed they must be tired from their duties, from being in front of the hot stove all day and from having to get up before everyone else in the morning, to go to market. As for those who misunderstood that she was infected with tuberculosis, she thought to herself that perhaps it was her good fortune, because she could have more time for herself and could eat as much or as little as she pleased without having to have consideration for others at the same table. Instead of having to chat, she could reflect on the inner experience she had attained at the centre of her body as she ate.

The Great Abbot would constantly push her to progress in her meditation practice. He would ask her, "On the way to the refectory, do you still maintain your mind at the centre of your body?" This meant Chandra to keep her mind at the centre of the body the whole of the time, just in case he asked, throughout her waking hours. In such a way, her adeptness in meditation depthened until she was allotted one of the special meditation beds[2] in the meditation workshop. The so-called 'meditation beds' were rather like a personal platform just large enough to sit on cross-legged. They were considered a sign of honour, accorded only to those whose attainments deserved

1. In Buddhism purely practising monks are believed to yield tremendous merit to those who share gifts with them.
2. The so-called '*Kard Roo*' beds were allocated only to those meditators whose mind was immersed completely on the inner experience.

it. When the meditators used them for research at night, because the platforms were of the minimum size, they forced the meditators to sit bolt upright, because if one leaned even slightly to either side, one would touch the mosquito net and would be bitten instantly. The upright sitting-posture Chandra acquired in her years of night-time research, was to stay with her *even* until her old age.

To qualify for such work, the meditator had to bring their mind so firmly to a standstill that their mind would break free of their physical body, unifying instead with the body of enlightenment — letting go of external knowledge to become immersed in internal knowledge for as long as the research session lasted. Thus, those able to do such research had to have a mind of the utmost purity and power. They had to have a faculty of seeing and knowing that was inordinately precise allowing them to understand in depth the nature of life and the world.

Chandra had never had the wish to settle down and have a family like her contemporaries. Although she couldn't become a monk, still she wanted to make the utmost devotion to Buddhism possible for her, and become a nun taking vows of celibacy. Once Chandra had come to the end of her month of leave – when all things being equal she would have to go back to her domestic duties — she made up her mind never to return. She divulged her intention to Upāsika Thongsuk, saying, "You know? I'm *not* going back."

Upāsika Thongsuk said, "I was thinking the same. Let's ordain as nuns instead."

"And how are we going to afford that?"

"How about renting[1] the robes we need for ordination?"

Even the lack of the necessary requisites could not stand in the way of their determined wish. They shaved each others' heads and ordained that very evening. Their decision to ordain brought a favourable response from the Great Abbot because he hadn't wanted them to go home at the end of the month either. He was reassured that his 'volunteer soldiers' had now become 'regulars'.

The next morning Khun Nai Liap called at the temple to fetch Chandra home, but was taken aback at Chandra's transformation — no more long hair, pure white robes and a complexion more radiant than ever. Khun Nai Liap guessed that Chandra had intended this all along, but was afraid to say anything out of consideration for the Great Abbot. She just glared at Chandra without saying anything. Later when the Great Abbot had left the pavilion, she turned to Sister Chandra[2] and asked in genuine disbelief, "How come you said you'd come back? Why have you gone and ordained?" Khun Yay didn't reply but maintained noble silence. She was normally a person of few words anyway. In fact Khun Nai Liap had been very attached to her.

Keeping the pure Precepts of a nun, it was much easier for Khun Yay to study the high-level Dhamma that the Great Abbot taught. He had them conduct foundation research the Five Aggregates [*khandha*],

---

1. The obstacle of wanting to take ordination but not being able to afford the simple robes to allow one to do so was a symptom of the everyday hardships commonplace to people of that time.

2. From here on, Chandra, Mae Chee Chandra etc. will be referred to as 'Khun Yay', or 'Khun Yay Chandra' where necessary to distiguish her from other nuns.

the Twelve Spheres of Knowing [*āyatana*], the Eighteen Elements [*dhātu*], the Twenty-Two Faculties [*indriya*], the Four Noble Truths [*ariyasacca*] and the Twelve Links of Dependent Origination [*pāṭiccasamuppada*]. With no books on her shelves, all Khun Yay's knowledge arose from *seeing* these things for herself. The more she practised, the more her knowledge extended. The more she researched, the more she saw. She discovered many aspects of the knowledge beyond the miraculous. Some of the things she learned can never be revealed until the time is appropriate. Eventually, without reading a single word, Khun Yay took her place in the ranks as a sage of high Dhamma attainment.

6

The Meditation Workshop

> "There are certain monks and Brahmins in this
> world who strive until they have uprooted the defile-
> ments. With perseverance in their striving, avoiding
> recklessness, they apply their skilfulness of mind and
> can attain psychical powers. When their mind is
> concentrated they can attain psychical powers, such
> as: one person can become many or many can become
> one, can appear or disappear at will, walking through
> walls as if walking through empty space, popping
> up from the ground or sinking into it, diving up out
> of the water or walking on it as if walking on solid
> earth, floating in the air like a bird, able to touch the
> sun or the moon with their own hands, able to reach
> the Brahma world with their physical body."
>
> *Sampasadiya Sutta*

The meditation workshop or 'rong-ngahn-tam-vi-
jja' was a large building, open inside except for a
long thin partition which ran down the length of
the building. At that time there were about thirty
monks meditating together on one side and about
thirty nuns and unordained laywomen on the other. Those meditating on one side of the partition
were unable to see those on the other. The partition
was designed to prevent monks and nuns being
a visual distraction to one another. Monks and

47

nuns thus had no contact with one another, hardly knowing one other. The Great Abbot would sit on the monks' side. There was a small hole perforated in the partition close to the Great Abbot's sitting position, to allow him to give instructions to those on both sides of the partition simultaneously. Only his face could be seen on the female side.

In peacetime, the meditators took it in turn to meditate in four hour shifts throughout the day. However, during the Second World War, this was reduced to four shifts per day, each six hours long. The first shift would sit from six in the evening until midnight, being replaced by the second shift from midnight to six in the morning. The first shift would return to meditate from six in the morning until noon and the second shift would return to sit from noon until six in the evening. The two shifts meditated alternately in this way so that there was meditation research being done twenty-four hours a day.

Khun Yay was selected as head of the late shift because she was seen as the most determined and was also of strong health. Even though she looked slightly built, she was earnest in everything she turned her hand to. She may have sat for meditation no longer than the others, but when she sat, she didn't move. She sat as if sitting to the death each time – without any more feeling for her body at all. All she registered were the experiences she plumbed from the inside. At the end of the six hour shift, the others in the shift would vacate the room immediately, but Khun Yay lingered on to hear what instruction the Great Abbot would have for the incoming shift for a further half-an-hour or so.

She would meditate with them as they started out on their new task for a while, before retiring from the workshop.

Even outside the room, she still maintained the subtlety of her mind as she was going about her personal chores. On the outside her body moved about its tasks, but on the inside her mind remained steadfastly focussed on inner wisdom. When it was time to go on shift, the others would turn up at the last moment, but Khun Yay would be there fifteen minutes before time, in order to hear the conclusions the Great Abbot made at the end of the outgoing shift in case there was something she could learn from. This is why it is said that of all the meditators, it was Khun Yay who absorbed most of the knowledge known to the Great Abbot. She let no meditation knowledge pass her by unheeded. She knew how each session began and ended — and even how it was transmitted to the next shift.

In those days it was routine for the Great Abbot to train his meditators to explore the realms of heaven and hell. However, those allowed to study in such a way had to be earnest and self-motivated to develop their own adeptness in 'seeing and knowing' to keep up with the depth of questions he was asking. If anyone was not diligent and focussed, the Great Abbot would reprimand them with the word 'embers!' – because embers have to be poked and prodded continually if you are going to rely on them to keep a fire going. Similarly, the 'embers' amongst the meditators needed continual prodding from the Abbot to make any progress in their meditation at all. Khun Yay, however, had never let herself be chided with the word 'embers!'

throughout the Great Abbot's life — like the legendary 'thoroughbred' of the Buddhist Scriptures which seeing its fellow horses whipped already learns its lesson.[1] It doesn't have to be whipped itself.

While doing research, Khun Yay Chandra and Khun Yay Thongsuk discovered a technique by which they could reap untold merit by offering sustenance directly to the Lord Buddha's body of enlightenment in Nirvana. They started a tradition of offering sustenance[2] in this way, to the Buddhas of the past, present and future, ceremonially once a month and as a way of performing 'grace' before every meal. In fact, this tradition in its superficial form was already present in Thai tradition — usually consisting merely of putting food on the shrine as an offering to the Lord Buddha. However, in the Dhammakāya Tradition, making this offering through meditation was to become an identifying feature of the tradition down to the present day.

One day some supporters offered the Great Abbot a rare fan made of peacock feathers. It was a very beautiful one and he brought it to the meditation workshop as prize someone in the 'workshop group' could win by drawing lots. At that time there were more than a hundred in the meditation workshop. The fan would be the prize for the most adept meditator. Although he knew the one worthy of winning it should be Khun Yay, he democratically allowed everyone in the workshop the chance to draw lots for it, as a test of their psychic feats. He merely made the wish to himself that the most accomplished would be the one to receive the prize. Khun Yay

---

1. Patoda Sutta A.ii.114   2. *Puja kao phra*

felt deeply that this fan belonged to her and meditating, made the silent wish that she would receive the fan.

That day Khun Yay was the last in the room to draw her lot – but strangely the winning lot evaded the hands of everyone else in the room. Once Khun Yay had picked the lot, she had someone else unroll it and read it out (because she couldn't read it for herself). She had won the fan through her psychic ability. Everybody was amused saying, "Her surname is '*khonnokyoong*' (meaning peacock feather) and she has been the one to win the peacock-feather fan!" The fan, however, was to stay with her only a few hours, because Khun Yay Thongsuk came asking after it. Khun Yay Thongsuk wanted to give the fan as a meritorious gift. Khun Yay wanted the merit *more* than the fan so gladly gave it to her old teacher. In fact it wasn't just the fact that Khun Yay Thongsuk had been her teacher. If *anyone* came asking for anything she had, she would give things away without a glimmer of regret. She loved to give more than to hoard. She didn't care for the external trappings of wealth, but only for the inner wealth of Dhamma attainment."

Everyone, even the Great Abbot, knew mundane things were the last thing on Khun Yay's mind and one day he tested her with a new sort of question. While they were sitting doing meditation research on an advanced topic, suddenly he changed the subject and asked Khun Yay, "What's so tasty about salted fish?"[1] For once, Khun Yay fell into a stunned silence. She didn't

---

1. in Thai *pla salit*

know where to start answering such a question. Usually, the Great Abbot would ask only about advanced metaphysics. However, when he asked about salted fish she had no idea how to answer. Normally she would just eat her food dutifully without ever thinking whether it was tasty or not. She ate merely to fill her stomach, to keep herself going and to gain the strength to do her meditation research. She had thus never noticed what was 'tasty' about salted fish!

Meditators at Wat Paknam practised strictly according to the Great Abbot's guidelines. His disciples were inspired to the degree that allowed Dhammakåya to spread to nearly every province in Thailand. Chosen disciples such as Khun Yay Thongsuk and Khun Yay Thean Theerawat were given a small amount of money by the abbot and sent to preach in more than eighteen provinces, some as far away as Chiangmai.

The same could not be said of Khun Yay. She never left the temple to go anywhere else. She would do nothing but meditate, day and night, continuously. Other researchers would leave the temple to make visits and call on friends, but Khun Yay had no money, no friends and no remaining relatives living in Bangkok. She had nothing to distract her from the meditation. She meditated dedicatedly and skilfully every day, arriving punctually for every session.

Nonetheless, someone once *did* invite Khun Yay to make a visit to Bangkok on the other side of the river. Khun Yay went to ask the Great Abbot's permission first. The Great Abbot was not enthusiastic about her going, afraid that she might meet circumstances along the way that would detract from the subtlety of her mind. Thus he said, "If there's something special that you *want,* just visualize it at your centre." Thus she didn't go, but imagined the thing she wanted to buy at her centre instead. The very next morning, miraculously, a stranger came and offered her just the thing she had been imagining.

On another occasion, when it came to the durian season, Khun Yay secretly hankered after a taste of durian. The Great Abbot knew what was on her mind and said, "If it's durian you want, you'll find it at the centre of your stomach. If that's what you want to eat, then just imagine it at the centre of your stomach."

She tried imagining the durian at the centre of her body and again, the next morning, someone she had never seen before brought durian to offer everyone at the temple. She came to the conclusion that the centre of the body must be the origin of all success in life. If one's mind is focussed at one's centre, fulfilment can be achieved without having to go the lengths of looking elsewhere.

Despite Khun Yay's youthfulness she practised seriously, like an elder — used to being ever-prepared with her meditation prowess. She would be at the right hand of the Great Abbot whenever he needed to call upon her. Apart from having inner attainments unexcelled by others, she was also someone contented with little. She didn't hoard possessions and she was not gregarious by nature. Her uncomplicated approach to the world allowed her mind to remain still the whole of the time, engrossed with the Dhamma both by day and by night. It was for all these reasons that she was trusted by the Great Abbot. She was the one he entrusted as the guardian of the rare crystal balls used when doing research. She would give the whole of herself to any meditation task set by the abbot and wouldn't allow herself to deviate from what he had asked of her (like some people who became distracted onto things not required of them). He had had her find the afterlife destinations of so many people in heaven and hell that she was inordinately accurate. If she made mistakes, she never made them twice. She was autodidactic in many respects. Even when imprecision was rife amongst others in the meditation workshop, she never took other people as her standard.

It was no surprise that she was accepted as the most accomplished. Whenever the Abbot asked her and question or requested her to do anything, she could easily do his bidding.[1] Nothing the Great Abbot challenged her to do was beyond her ability. If she was asked to look for the afterlife destination of the departed, she could do it. She could calculate the amount of merit people had performed. She could look into the future or the past.

It was Khun Yay's attentiveness and devotion to her Master's command that lead the Great Abbot to compliment her, "My daughter Chandra is number one — second to none," in front of all the others who did the meditation research with her. This was a complement which the Great Abbot was to give only once throughout his life.

---

1. With the exception of the example mentioned above

7

The Real War to be Fought

"Iddhivisayo ajintayadayo"

*The nature of those with mental powers is
beyond the speculation of conceptual thought.*

Those with mental powers are those whose mind is
already still and free from thought. Such a mind is one
able to study heaven, hell or Nirvana at first hand. It
is impossible for mere unenlightened worldlings to
estimate the potential of those with mental powers.
The power of the mind at a standstill is without limit.
Thus it is no surprise that the Buddhist scriptures
describe many miraculous events surrounding those
who had already managed to train their minds to great
purity. Not only monks and nuns, but even laypeople
who had trained their minds to the same extent had
many miracles surrounding them. Lady Visākhā[1], a
stream-enterer since the age of seven, had strength
exceeding that of five elephants. The laywoman Mā-
tika Māta[2] was able to read the minds of others and
to recollect her own and others' previous lifetimes.
All of this was attributable to mental powers coming
as a byproduct of having trained themselves long and
hard in meditation. Once able to master one's own
mind, it becomes possible to have control over the
things around one whether it be things in the mind,
our bodies or the environment. All eventually come

1. DhA.i.409   2. DhA.i.293

under one's control. Once the mind becomes lighter and more subtle, the physical body can become light and subtle too, even allowing the meditator to float in the air.

Khun Yay was no exception. Because she had striven in meditation for a long time, her mind was very subtle the whole time and she was able to do exceptional things *as a result* of her meditation.

Khun Yay had been doing meditation research with the Great Abbot for two years when the Second World War broke out. In World War II, Bangkok was occupied by soldiers of the Axis — more than a million in all. Thailand became like a barracks used as a hub by the Axis for attacks against Burma and India. The Allies bombed Bangkok ceaselessly. In spite of the bombing, the Great Abbot refused to evacuate the temple. He said that if the worst came to the worst he would die there with his temple. Moreover, he intensified his activities owing to the increased number of temple-goers. Wat Paknam was located only a "stone's throw" away from the lock between the mouth of the Bhasicharoen Canal and the Canal of Greater Bangkok. This was a place of strategic significance and a target for Allied bombing. The Great Abbot had unshakable faith that the omnipotence of the *Dhammakāya* would protect Wat Paknam and its congregation from the bombs. The Great Abbot's confidence was not unfounded and in reality, neither Wat Paknam nor the adjacent locks were ever to sustain bomb damage.

Temple attendance increased because Wat Paknam gained a reputation for safety in time of air raids. The public believed that the Great

Abbot had some sort of magic power and before long, whenever air-raid sirens were sounded, the people of Bhasicharoen would hasten to the temple precincts rather than shelter in air-raid bunkers. The Great Abbot would have the meditators check when the squadrons of bombers would arrive on their bomb-runs against Bangkok. He'd ask, "What time will they drop their bombs today?" Knowing the time, when he heard the distant explosions of bombs falling, he'd remain unmoved and say, "Go and intercept those bombs in case they harm somebody. Have them fall in the ocean or in uninhabited areas instead."

The Great Abbot employed his adepts to help the national effort and mankind as a whole, without taking sides. He meditated to bring an end to the conflict — to restore peace. He had his meditators make their minds subtle and use the power of the Dhammakāya to overcome the problems. He used the powers of meditation to cause the bomb-aimers to see their strategic targets as forests or open sea so that they wouldn't drop their bombs there. They made the forests and sea appear like cities to the bomb-aimers so that they emptied their bomb bays without harming anyone.

Indeed, in 1941, many of the Bangkok newspapers gave front-page coverage to the manifestation of miracles at Wat Paknam. One particular incident which riveted press such as *Vipassana Banteungsarn* was an air-raid on Bangkok — the target of which was the Phraputha-yodfa-chulalok Bridge. Wat Paknam was within striking distance of this target. At that time the inhabitants of the neighbourhood gazed skyward and were surprised to see large numbers of nuns from Wat Paknam floating in the air, intercepting the bombs and apparently[1] patting them with their bare hands, again to fall harmlessly in the water or uninhabited areas of forest. So many people saw the heroic efforts of the nuns with their own eyes that the renown of the miracles of the Great Abbot of Wat Paknam spread far and wide. Everybody saw the efforts by the Great Abbot to reduce bloodshed and encourage harmony amongst his fellow men.

For most people, it would have been arduous to spend wartime meditating for such long hours and under such great pressure. It would have affected the health even of the strongest person — but for Khun Yay, the wartime years were nothing special. Khun Yay had no fear of the bombing. She never missed even a shift of meditation research despite the chaos of the times. She felt it was her pleasure simply to have the chance to further her mastery of the Dhammakåya knowledge. Because of shortage of cloth at that time, most of the nuns meditating were reduced to rags. The once plentiful food became scarce. There was massive flooding throughout the country. Khun Yay didn't let these things perturb her meditation.

The Great Abbot had long been renowned for the special compassion he displayed towards foreigners. If any foreigner were to attain Dhammakåya in meditation, he could not cease to express his happiness for days upon end. The Great Abbot extended this same compassion to the warring nations of the War. In spite of the hostilities and the obvious temptation for nationalist feeling, the Great Abbot and his meditators, regarded a world at war with impartiality.

---

1. In actual fact, they used their meditation rather than their hands, to avert the bombs.

Neither nationality nor the occupation of Thailand caused them to view one side or the other as their enemies. They saw all humans as equal and prayed for harmony and an end to the hostilities without bloodshed. Indeed, the standard blessing he gave to all who attended the temple was that all prosper, that the rice ripen in the fields, that the rain fall according to season and that men everywhere give up fighting amongst themselves.

The most important contribution which Khun Yay was to make was to protect Thailand from the atomic bomb. At a time shortly before the end of the war, one member of the 'workshop group' had the vision while meditating of a new kind of weapon, a bomb, being built by the Allies to put an end to the war in Asia — and that the Allies were planning to use this weapon against Bangkok. Khun Yay was told to check what would happen if such a bomb should drop on Bangkok. She saw in meditation, that the whole of the city would be wiped out, razed to the ground. She told the Abbot that everybody would be killed and the city would be as flat as the skin of a drum. The Great Abbot then commanded the temple's treasurer, a man of middle age, to take all the temple's assets and get away from the temple — to go away as far from the city as he could in seven days. If the Abbot's efforts met with success, the treasurer could return as if nothing had happened. The Abbot spoke of this matter with no-one else. The Abbot locked the doors of the workshop allowing no-one to enter or leave. Food and drink would be sent through the letter-box. When the bomb siren sounded, some meditators in the room ran about in terror. Khun Yay was not afraid of the bombs and kept on meditating. The 'workshop group' sat down in earnest for meditation in order to try and save the country. For a reason known only to the Great Abbot and his meditators, the bomber and the bombs never arrived in Bangkok. The Allies had for some reason changed their minds. It had taken seven days of perpetual meditation behind locked doors to influence that decision for the sake of their fellow men.

After the Second World War had come to an end there was no real threat to national security any more, but Khun Yay didn't reduce the effort she made in her meditation. She was to continue with her meditation research. She remained unexcelled in her precise inner knowledge of phenomena, wholesome [*kusala*], unwholesome [*akusala*] and neutral [*abyakata*]. She learned about the battle since ancient times between the wholesome and the unwholesome – and how these affected lives even down to the present day. Seeing these things, she honed her mind to a more and more perfect standstill to do battle with the Māra, knowing that the defilements in the mind all originated from the work of the Māra. She thought of nothing else but how to forge ahead in meditation to the point the Utmost Dhamma[1] could be attained. Often in the company of her nearest disciples, Khun Yay would tell them, "It is not for me to enter Nirvana yet. I have to finish off the Māras first."

The Great Abbot of Wat Paknam said that the origin of all the suffering of living beings is the Māra. The obstacles we habitually come up against, every time we attempt to perform an act of virtue, come

1. *tee sut haeng thamm*: a point where Mara has been defeated, eradicating all suffering in the universe at its roots.

from the Māra, preventing us from pursuing Perfections[1] in convenience. Māras are mentioned in many places in the Buddhist Scriptures, especially the constant battle between the wholesome and the unwholesome, good and evil, virtue and demerit, the light side and the dark side, knowledge and ignorance, purity and impurity. The fight goes on the whole time, on the battlefields of the body, mind and the environment. The two opponents, Dhamma and *adhamma*[2] compete the whole of the time for control of existence at all levels. The Great Abbot of Wat Paknam maintained that for as long as Dhamma didn't manage to reach back to the origin of the suffering, ousting those responsible for producing such suffering, there would be no way of stopping the suffering from the world of beings. There would be no end to the inflicting of harm. The Great Abbot saw all this through his meditation, by the power of the knowledge of *Dhammakāya* and consequently devoted his entire life to bringing the mind to a standstill in order to make unerring progress on the central axis.

The Great Abbot would always say that waging war in the human realm was never justifiable because hatred is never appeased by hatred.[3] In such conflicts one was not fighting against one's real enemy. One's real enemy is the defilements in one's mind, especially the Māra — the source of the defilements in one's mind, whether it be greed, hatred or delusion. Only in the absence of such defilements could real peace

1. Good deeds pursued until they become an engrained part of body and mind.
2. the antithesis of virtue representing all that is bad, unjust and unwholesome
3. Dhammapada verse 5

come about in the world. Although the behaviours done under the influence of the defilements[1] are visible to the outside world, the defilements themselves were visible only to the Eye of the *Dhammakāya*. The more subtle one's attainment in meditation, the more thoroughly one would be able to identify the remaining defilements in mind, body or environment. This was the origin of the quest to reach the Utmost Dhamma. Reaching this destination, one would be able to extinguish all suffering at its source. For as long as one had not reached this destination, one would have to remain the slave of the Māras. The Māras force people to think unwholesomely, say and do unwholesome things. They thrust old age, sickness and death on all — forcing everyone to get mixed up in unwholesome behaviours. They throw the natural environment and the climate out of balance, so that the rain doesn't fall according to season, so that the economy goes into recession, so that famine, drought and plague hamper peoples' lives, to exacerbate wars. Thus one has to reach the Utmost Dhamma to beat the Māra at their source. This was why Khun Yay spent the whole of her life researching in meditation, by day and by night. However, there was only so much one could achieve in a single lifetime.

1.the mental impurities of greed, hatred and delusion that are the seeds of unwholesomeness of body, speech and mind.

8

The Passing of the Pioneer Root Teachers

Sappuriso ca kho bhikkhave   *kataññū hoti katavedī*
sabbhi h'etaṃ bhikkhave   *upaññataṃ yadidaṃ*
kataññutā katavedita.   *Kevala esa bhikkhave*
sappurisabhūmi yadidaṃ   *kataññutā katavedita ti*

O! Monks! The Noble person is someone who both appreciates his debt of gratitude to others and repays that debt of gratitude. Such a person is praised by the noble ones. O! Monks! All forms of gratitude are the foundation of nobility.

A.i.61

About 1954, the Great Abbot had his students summoned from throughout the temple, saying that within five years he was going to die, but that all should continue to propagate the method of Dhammakāya meditation throughout the world — and that it would be very important and beneficial for mankind. His major concerns at that time were that the building work should be completed before his death, that offering of food to the monks should be sufficient and that the study of Buddhist Scripture should be maintained. He appealed to all to continue persevering with the activities he had set in motion. He said that before long the temple would be enlarged, even though he would no longer be present. His disciples pleaded for him to stay on longer, but he said that he must surely die. Everyone present immediately knew how concerned the Great Abbot was for the welfare of the tradition to have publicly appealed to his disciples to take responsibility for the work — especially for perpetuating and spreading the *Dhammakāya* tradition.

The Great Abbot instructed Khun Yay to stay and teach the knowledge of *Dhammakāya* at Wat Paknam while waiting for a successor to arrive. He ordered:

> "(Daughter) Chandra! Don't be in a hurry to die! Don't give up the teaching life for the seclusion of the forests! After my passing the others will have to rely on you to teach the knowledge of *Dhammakāya* and keep them on the straight and narrow path. If you don't teach them, they will fall victim to the work of the Māra."

By 1957 the Great Abbot's condition had worsened. He knew he would not live much longer. Even when the Great Abbot was severely ill, his mind was still engrossed with Dhamma and meditation research. Every evening he would call the monks to meditate near him for one or two hours. Khun Yay was, as a nun, not permitted to care for him when he was bedridden. All she could do was note his symptoms from a distance. At night he required everyone to meditate. He never rested from teaching meditation until the last day of his life. Before passing away, he chided his disciples saying,

> "Our reach is too short. We cannot beat Māra this lifetime. We are still in their clutches."

His words, however, were not meant as an insult to the meditation ability of his disciples. He didn't mean to accuse them of failure. He simply wanted to make sure they knew that the work was not finished so that no one should rest on their laurels until victory was achieved.

Before the Great Abbot died, he made prophecies about the temple. He said that Wat Paknam would become very popular and there would be many new students coming to join the congregation. He ordered the nuns not to cremate his body but rather to embalm it. His entombed corpse would continue to ensure the prosperity of the temple — 'nurturing' those who lived on by attracting pilgrims to visit Wat Paknam and pay homage. Instructions for meditation would be received from a tape recording of his voice in the chamber where his body lay. Pilgrims would thus continue to make donations for the prosperity of the temple.

Something had changed since the Great Abbot had fallen ill. He had no time to lead his students in the meditation workshop. The abbot had no time to train new workshop meditators either. Without the Great Abbot's involvement, the educational emphasis of the temple swung more and more in the direction of the academic studies to the neglect of the meditation research. Indeed, from that time forth, Wat Paknam verily became one of the national centres for Buddhist scriptural study. By the time of the Great Abbot's death, most of the masters of meditation had fled the temple, to live elsewhere, away from the temple in isolation. The only ones left were some nuns who still practised at the temple and followed the original pattern of teaching taught by the Great Abbot. His last words had been:

> "Carry on doing the work as if I were alive.
> Never stop meditating. Keep doing good and
> continue to support the monks."

The Great Abbot passed away on the third of February 1959 at the age of seventy-three. Despite the majesty of a lifetime's ministry, when he passed away it was only pitiful few of his disciples, principally the nuns who had stayed at his side throughout his ministry, who continued with his mission in its original spirit. Other followers tried to recapture the meditation experience they had attained with the Great Abbot by leaving the temple and retreating to the forests to meditate.

After the Great Abbot's passing, Khun Yay remained at Wat Paknam still living in the same small *kuti* with Khun Yay Thongsuk. It never escaped Khun Yay's mind that Khun Yay Thongsuk was behind all the success in her own Dhamma career. This led Khun Yay Chandra to respect Khun Yay Thongsuk and hold her in the highest esteem. Throughout Khun Yay Chandra's stay at Wat Paknam, they had stayed together — sometimes like elder and younger sisters, sometimes like teacher and pupil.

When the Great Abbot had been alive, Khun Yay Thongsuk had been entrusted by the Great Abbot with the task of spreading Dhamma far and wide to all the provinces of Thailand. Often Khun Yay Thongsuk would have to travel far away from the temple to give sermons. She would be away from the meditation workshop for days at a time. In such a case, Khun Yay would slip out of touch with the progress in the meditation research so it was up to

Khun Yay Chandra to bring her up to date with progress in the research whenever she returned. Being kept in touch by Khun Yay Chandra in this way allowed Khun Yay Thongsuk to excel both in research and in propagation of the Dhamma. The knowledge of *Dhammakāya* thus began to take a foothold in the provinces. When Khun Yay Thongsuk was still in good health, she would travel all over Thailand teaching meditation for people of all walks of life. Consequently, she had students all over the country. She would return *exhausted* from her trips. Her time at the temple was a time when she could recover from her voyaging and Khun Yay Chandra was able to wait on her, to help make her time back at the temple a time to cherish. In return for being brought up to date on the meditation research, Khun Yay Thongsuk would tell of her adventures in the provinces.

In 1960, not long after the death of the Great Abbot, Khun Yay Thongsuk herself was struck down by cervical cancer. When her symptoms were at their worst, Khun Yay Thongsuk would be admitted to Sirirat Hospital. When the symptoms were less aggravated, she would be allowed to convalesce at her *kuti* at Wat Paknam. Eventually, when the symptoms became so bad that the hospital gave her no further hope, she was left with no alternative but to remain at the *kuti*. The terminal symptoms of cancer were horrifying, stinking blood and lymph fluid poured from her wound. The stench was so strong that the formerly numerous volunteers looking after her dwindled until she was abandoned by all except for Khun Yay Chandra. Khun Yay Chandra saw this as being the chance in some small way to repay her debt of gratitude to Khun Yay Thongsuk, her first teacher. Khun Yay Chandra was the one to launder her clothes by hand and to find appropriate food for her teacher. Khun Yay never felt demoralized by her tasks and never let her repugnance for her dying teacher's symptoms distance her from her gratitude.

She would listen with patience when Khun Yay Thongsuk called out deliriously at the height of her fever. Although the doctor might have her administer medicine at certain times of the day, such as before or after meals, that was not to say that the patient would be *willing* to take the medicine at those times. She had to use tact and observe both the mood and the symptoms of the patient who was often reluctant to take the medicine *at all*. Often when Khun Yay Thongsuk saw Khun Yay Chandra pouring out the medicine, she would cry out in her fever, "I don't want to take that medicine anymore. What's the use of it?" Knowing that the time was not right, Khun Yay Chandra would retreat and wait compassionately for her teacher to give her the chance to relieve her of at least *part* of her suffering. Both knew the cancer to be terminal, but Khun Yay Chandra didn't allow the fact to diminish the care she accorded to her teacher. Whenever the delirium abated or her patient was in better spirits, Khun Yay Chandra would be back at her side with the bottle of medicine whether by day or by night.

Particularly in the olden days, cancer was a terrifying disease. There was no effective medicine against it *or* the terrible smell of festering tumours it caused. Khun Yay had to clean up after her teacher's discharges, give her a blanket bath and wash her clothes. She brought perfumed ointment to help hide the smell — at least to preserve Khun Yay Thongsuk's dignity when students from all over the country came to see her on sick visits.

One day, after Khun Yay Thongsuk had visited the restroom, she smiled reassuringly, but said to Khun Yay Chandra in a perfectly matter-of-fact voice, "The cancer has now eaten through my intestines. You alone will be with me as I die. The others won't want to be there." When it came to her final hour, Khun Yay Thongsuk lay dying with her head in Khun Yay Chandra's lap. Indeed, they *were* left alone. Although the disease was wreaking its worst, Khun Yay Thongsuk's eyes were alert and open. She informed Khun Yay Chandra, "My time has come. I can see Buddha images all around me." Khun Yay Chandra listened without any sign of grief, replying, "Sister! Cast yourself into Nirvana." Such words made sense only between adepts of meditation. Khun Yay Thongsuk passed away peacefully there in Khun Yay Chandra's lap.

Khun Yay organised a funeral of dramatic scale for her teacher and sister in the Dhamma, with three days of ceremony. The chanting was held at Wat Paknam and the cremation at Wat Apsornsuwan, with the subsequent floating away of her ashes on the water. Khun Yay was able to borrow the funerary altar previously used for the funeral of the well-known princess of King Rama V. It was an elegant and well-organised ceremony.

9
Teacher in Her Own Right

Ye jhānapasutā dhīrā   nekhammuupasame ratā
Devāpi tesaṃ pihayanti   sambuddhānaṃ satimataṃ

Humans and angels alike delight at the sage who strives to bring forth the absorptions, contented with the peacefulness arising from renunciation, endowed with mindfulness and wisdom.

Dh.51

After Khun Yay Thongsuk's passing, Khun Yay stayed on at Wat Paknam, out of a sense of duty to the dying words of the Great Abbot. Even ten years later, many people continued to express the view that Khun Yay Chandra would be no good as a meditation teacher because she spoke so little compared with the late Khun Yay Thongsuk. However, Khun Yay had confidence in herself that somehow her ability would be of help to the world. Khun Yay had never been trained to be a preacher of Buddhism, only as a deep meditator. She had no skill in public-speaking but her mastery was the internal strength built through years of intensive meditation. She had a very decisive personality. Assured of the existence of the *Dhammakāya* through her own meditational experience, she never used flowery words to attract others' interest in meditation. Instead she would merely lead them to become assured themselves, through their own meditational experience. She would tell them, "meditate and you will find out for yourself!" The directness and harshness of her words cut through the excuses of many people and inspired them to come and meet her again.

Although Khun Yay was never the one teach – she got down to the task of teaching beginning with the residual students trained up by Khun Yay Thongsuk.[1] If anyone wanted to study Buddhism with her, she would instruct them in meditation – and have them meditate regularly. She wouldn't engage them in fruitless conversation. *Practice* was the watchword rather than chatting. Once they started to have inner experience such as the inner spheres or the inner bodies for themselves, they would understand the knowledge of *Dhammakāya* for themselves. Many were able to attain the *Dhammakāya*.

At that time Khun Yay lived in a rickety old wooden *kuti* which had originally been three storeys high, but looked from the outside like it had only a single storey. It was this *kuti* she had shared with Khun Yay Thongsuk. The stilts between the first floor and the ground were about four feet high – leaving space enough to crawl or sit but not to stand. The ground floor was 'paved' with wooden boards but was again swept spotless. People came there to meditate – the so-called 'downstairs'. The first floor was the most spacious part of the house. Along one wall of the room was a shrine table with a Buddha image, storage cupboards and a second shrine table with a picture of Khun Yay Thongsuk, her teacher. The other side of the room was Khun Yay's living space. It was where she meditated, slept, received guests and did the ceremony for offering

---

1. An achievement also described in the academic writing of McDaniel (2006, p.110), na Songkhla (1999, p.259) and Heikkilä-Horn (1996).

sustenance to the Lord Buddha each first Sunday of the month. In a small cabinet next to where she sat to receive guests were various sorts of medicines she would dispense to those who came to her with medical problems. The medicine bottles were arranged in neat lines. Almost in the centre of the room there was the so-called 'headless' pillar which didn't quite reach the ceiling. The third storey (or second floor of the house) was like a landing one metre higher than the first floor. The second floor was in fact the ceiling of the downstairs kitchen which had been made high enough to stand up in.

Early in the day, at 04.00 a.m. she would get up early to meditate for herself until breakfast time. At about 08.30 a.m. she would sit again for meditation, but this time in order to teach others. Whether the people attending were many or few, she would teach meditation. No matter who was visiting her that morning, she had a stock phrase which she always used:

> "If you're in no particular hurry, put aside your other commitments. Let's sit and clarify our minds for a moment and *then* talk."

Newcomers would agree to meditate reluctantly. Most of the people who came to visit her in those days were middle-aged people with their own families. Most were of working age. She used thirty years of meditation experience to teach others to meditate. Some of her visitors who had a baseline of virtue in their lives and who had some experience of meditation with the Great Abbot attained inner brightness of mind immediately with her. Finally, if those people needed any advice from her, she would give it as part of the meditation instruction in the final ten minutes of the session, speaking while both of them had their eyes closed. Such advice seemed to be absorbed by them at a deeper level – because it was advice given at a time when the mind was refined by meditation. This was how Khun Yay gave training to those coming to her.

Khun Yay had her own way of spreading the Dhamma. Apart from teaching meditation to interested students she would always be available to alleviate the suffering of those who came to her with problems of life or health. They would seek Khun Yay's help when their children or grandchildren were declared beyond cure by hospitals. Some came to her to have her find missing persons. Some wanted to dedicate merit for relatives who had passed away. Khun Yay had her way of making sure that even those who came to her for other reasons got a knowledge of meditation to take home with them.

She would use the knowledge of *Dhammakāya* to help all-comers as much as practically possible treating all as equals, with a mind filled with compassion. Even though some came to her without treating her with any respect or even those merely wishing to 'try it on' she would still do her best to help them. Errands taking her to the heaven and hell realms were things that Khun Yay made look commonplace, more like walking from her *kuti* to other parts of the temple than traversing afterlife realms. Faced with the questioning of guests, she wouldn't do anything special. Just close her eyes for a moment, meditating to bring her into unity with the *Dhammakāya* within, until her faculty of 'seeing and knowing' expanded to the size of the Three

Realms – until the whole of the thirty-one realms was as a gooseberry in the palm of her hand. Closing her eyes to find the deceased in their afterlife destination seemed no more difficult than anyone else opening their eyes to look for a lost object in their room.

If the deceased had fallen into the hell realms, she would not beat around the bush with the guests who had asked her. She would tell them the karma they had done to deserve it in their most recent life. "Now they are in such-and-such a level of hell and are undergoing such-and-such a sort of retribution," or "Now they have exhausted their retribution in hell and have transmigrated to such-and-such a better existence." Her guests would thank her. Khun Yay would explain that they'd be best to perform a meritorious action and dedicate the merit for the benefit of the departed. For it to be effective, they'd have to purify their own minds too by meditating each day.

Often, if she helped a victim, she'd report that she had taught the deceased to meditate and had reminded them that if they omitted to meditate, they would fall back into the hell realms from whence they had come. Often the guests who came to visit her would be surprised to find that Khun Yay knew more about the unskilful actions of the deceased they did, even after having lived with them for years! Often they had seen only the good deeds the person had done before their demise.

There was once a certain couple who came to see Khun Yay for the first time. Once they had paid their respects to her, she started the conversation by saying, "It's about time you stopped betting on the horses." The husband appeared startled and looked daggers at his wife, thinking she had betrayed his vices to the nun behind his back. The wife protested, "Don't look at me like that. It's my first visit here too!" Khun Yay's tone of voice had been 'matter of fact' as if she was just complaining to no-one in particular – however, the strange thing was that her observations, even though only known to the doer, were accurate every time.

Another couple once came to ask her help. The wife was a teacher at Wat Bovornives School and was a regular disciple of Khun Yay. Her husband was also a good man, but extremely stubborn. He didn't believe in the existence of heaven or hell, but performed various sorts of meritorious actions just in case. He'd do chanting for an hour or maybe two every day – if hell turned out to be a reality, he'd be able to save himself from it.

That day he came asking Khun Yay, "Teacher! Something strange happened to me. If I may, I'd like to tell you about it, so you can say whether I've been imagining it or not." He settled into the story. "One night as I was lying outside on the balcony of our country house the moonlight was bright enough to see by. I saw something like a pillar of smoke slip up-wards between the gaps of the balcony floorboards coming together as a human figure as high as a tree. The figure then stepped away over the rooftops. I was able to see it with my own eyes. I've no idea what I've seen. Look! I've taken this story of mine to many temples already but I've never been given a satisfactory answer. Some tag the word 'probably' onto their answers. Some say I've been imagining things."

Khun Yay closed her eyes as she was listening to the

tale. Onlookers sitting within earshot, overhearing the blunt manner of the husband, wondered how Khun Yay would deal with the situation.

"So Teacher! What would *you* say it was that I've seen?" As soon as the man had finished his question, Khun Yay opened her eyes and looked at him, saying, "What you saw was a hungry-ghost [*peta*]. That hungry-ghost was one of your late relatives."

The man looked at her in angry disbelief before protesting, "No relative of mind would ever end up as hungry-ghost!"

Khun Yay didn't make any reaction to the man's childishness. With no sign of irritation, she continued to sit there impartially as was her normal manner. Even though he'd said he didn't believe her, he couldn't help mulling over the possibility of one of his relatives having become a hungry ghost. Khun Yay showed no sign of annoyance, but it was the onlookers who felt angry with the man *instead* for his lack of consideration for the nun – half anger and half curiosity to see how she was going to deal with the situation. She calmly explained, "Your relative was formerly the temple's MC but embezzled temple incomes for himself. When he died, that's why he has arisen as a hungry-ghost in his present lifetime."

"Impossible! There's no relative of mine who has ever been a temple MC. Teacher! If you're so smart, go ahead and tell me the relative's name!"

As usual, Khun Yay had nothing by way of untoward reactions. She told him calmly, "He went by the name of Rasamee."

"If it's the name 'Rasamee', its certainly no relative of mine. If it were my relative, they'd have a better name than that!" He raised his hands in a token gesture of prayer and left the *kuti* by the stairs.

He was not seen again until everyone had almost forgotten the incident. After several months, he came to see Khun Yay again and furtively admitted, "Well! I've been making some enquiries. It turns out that I *did* have a relative by that name. He was called Rasamee and he was the temple MC. He died long ago. Well! I can't pretend to know whether he embezzled temple funds – but *one* thing is for sure – there's *nothing* you're going to say that is convince me as to the existence of hungry ghosts!"

Some guests would come asking Khun Yay's advice whether to undergo an operation or not. For some of them Khun Yay would ask, "What's the point of you having the operation – you'll recover even without one." Often they'd protest that they'd already made an appointment with the surgeon. Khun Yay would say merely, "It's up to you. If you're going for the operation, then repeat the mantra '*Sammā-Arahaṃ*' to yourself as you do so." Later, after returning from the operation they came back to Khun Yay and admitted that once the doctor had opened them up during surgery, they couldn't find the alleged abnormality. Khun Yay would say humbly, "Well! At least now you know what it's like to have an operation!"

Khun Yay used the same principles she had learned from the Great Abbot of Wat Paknam to help alleviate the suffering of those who came to her for refuge. If the sick came to her, if they still had some remaining merit to remain alive, she would be able to help all of them to recover. This meant that there was a never ending stream of people seeking her out.

About six months after the death of Khun Yay Thongsuk, there was a palmist sitting in front of Khun Yay's small hut offering her his services free. He explained, "You will have a large number of new students and will be a refuge to thousands of people. "You can't expect me to believe that!" said Khun Yay. "I live alone and I have nothing. I have no students. I have nothing but this small *kuti*." As if in response to the Great Abbot's prophecy, a new generation of students interested in meditation started to come to Wat Paknam Bhasicharoen and sought out Khun Yay at her humble *kuti*. Khun Yay didn't think much of it, but remembering the Great Abbot's words, she started to teach them to the best of her ability.

After a while however, she had begun to realise that the prediction of the palmist was true. She started to have a growing number of students of an age young enough to be her own grandchildren. She had realised that this was the start of what the Great Abbot had meant when he had talked about 'taking meditation to the world'. She formed a small class of meditators and taught in her own hut. Around 1961, when Khun Yay was fifty-two years old her health started to suffer. She fell ill for many months and in the meantime, some of her students wrote her biography into a book. Although Khun Yay Chandra was not a 'teaching' meditation master, articles about her subsequently appeared in meditation books and popular Buddhist magazines. Of course, Khun Yay Thongsuk remained *more* famous than Khun Yay Chandra because she was a better speaker, going into such depth of details and meditation experience that she earned the respect of contemporary Buddhist scholars for the thoroughness of her metaphysical understanding — even though Khun Yay Thongsuk, like Khun Yay Chandra, had been illiterate.

As the number of her own students grew, the capacity of Khun Yay's rickety *kuti* was exceeded. There was no longer enough space for everybody to sit for meditation. The group who came to meditate with her raised 58,000 Baht from scratch, allowing them to build a two-storey house with a kitchen, a bathroom and a small front garden, within the compound of Wat Paknam. It was a purpose-built for meditation teaching — the first home of 'Dhammaprasit' — the precursor of the Dhammakāya Foundation.

The house was constructed with the engineering skills of the Ven. Narong Thitañāṇo and was given its name by Phrabhavanakosolthera. In the new house, Khun Yay retained her usual habits of cleanliness and orderliness. The group of students became known as the 'Students of Dhammaprasit house'. The number of Khun Yay's students grew rapidly as time went by. She continued to teach them meditation in great earnest.

When Khun Nai Liap was eighty-five years old, she would still come to Wat Paknam and whenever she met Khun Yay would remind her, "Sister Chandra! You said you'd come back afterwards but you never did." Even when Khun Nai Liap was on her deathbed, she had a servant invite Khun Yay to her home in order to make an offering to her for the last time, but as soon as she arrived said the same thing, "Sister Chandra! You said you'd come back afterwards but you never did," resignedly handing over a donation for Khun Yay for her personal use. It had never been Khun Yay's intention to be a maidservant for the rest of her life. Training a new generation of students and passing on the tradition to a successor was the mission the Great Abbot had left her with.

10
Training a Successor

Kāyasuciṃ, vācāsuciṃ   cetosuciṃ anāsavaṃ
Suciṃ soceyyasampannaṃ āhu ninhātapāpakan ti

*Those who are clean in body speech and mind, who are
free of mental defilements, endowed with cleanliness,
who are cleansed of all demerit — such people are recognized by the wise as being truly clean.*

A.i.273

There was a student of economics at Suan Kularb
School — one of the best secondary schools in
Bangkok — who had an insatiable appetite to
know about Buddhism and all things supernatu-
ral. The unanswered questions of 'Why we were
born' and 'What our purpose is in life' lingered
on unanswered in his mind. He didn't know
who to ask. Charming and talented in social af-
fairs. He was popular amongst friends and he
was a student found personable by all. However,
none of them could overlook this young man's
dedication to Buddhism and meditation. His
name was Chaiyaboon Sutthiphol. He was tall,
thin and wore dark glasses to alleviate a sensi-
tivity for bright sunlight. His spiritual questions
had been on his mind since the age of thirteen.

He had read a magazine called '*Vipassana Banteungsarn*' which retold the heroic efforts of Khun

Yay Chandra and Khun Yay Thongsuk during the War. The magazine even had pictures of the two nuns and others such as 'Kru Yannee'. The article told how they had averted the bombs dropped on Bangkok. The student figured that if Khun Yay were able to avert falling bombs, answering *his* questions should be a piece of cake. That was his prime mover in seeking out Khun Yay. However, strangely enough, even though the house he was living in at the time was in Thonburi near to Wat Paknam he never seemed to visit.

It was a full three years later when the student was nineteen, that he would have the opportunity to go to Wat Paknam again. On arrival, he still didn't know where to look for Khun Yay. As he was looking around the temple, he caught a glimpse of a wiry old nun who was standing in front of the building where Khun Yay Thongsuk had been commemorated. She had her back to him. The student didn't know her and she didn't know him. He had no way of telling whether it was the same person as he had seen in the magazine or not. Thus, the first day, although he had unwittingly come within speaking distance of Khun Yay, he had to go home disappointed. Trying to find her seemed to lead in circles. He didn't go to Wat Paknam again for a long time. He engrossed himself with his studies. His questions remained unanswered.

He started university, studying economics at Kasetsart University, Bangkok. In October 1963, during the vacation, he decided to go looking for Khun Yay at Wat Paknam again. Again, he asked after a nun called 'Mother Chandra', but no-one had heard of anyone by that name. Eventually he found someone who said that there was *no* 'Mother Chandra', there was only 'Teacher Chandra'. He thought it was probably someone else.

Nevertheless, the day was not wasted, because an aging monk spotted him and suggested he went and studied Dhamma with a monk called 'Acharn Veera' who was able to teach meditation as it had been taught by the late Great Abbot of Wat Paknam. That monk, Phrabhavanakosolthera (Veera Gaṇuttamo) allowed the student to sit by the loudspeaker from which one could hear what was going on inside the meditation workshop. The instructions were impossible for him to understand. They were talking about subtle things like alleviating human suffering, drought and famine. About having the rain fall according to season or healing peoples' diseases. Deep down inside, he liked listening to that sort of conversation, even though he didn't really understand it. It made him feel cool inside. He heard them talking about the Måras for hours at a time – and that was the thing really to impress him.

Next day, the student came back to the temple again and sat listening at the loudspeaker. He did this each day for a fortnight, but he still hadn't forgotten his wish to meet with Khun Yay. He asked a young man of approximately the same age sitting by him, whether he knew 'Mother Chandra'. The man said there was no 'Mother Chandra' only a 'Teacher Chandra'. "Can you take me to see Teacher Chandra then?" he asked, on the off-chance that it be the same person. This time he was introduced to Khun Yay, on the steps of the mausoleum for the tomb of the Great Abbot.

Khun Yay had a radiant complexion and a smile on her face. At that time she was fifty-three — but even though she looked thin and unimposing with no special presence, she had a sparkle in her eye that set her apart from other people. She had eyes which spoke of deep compassion, determination and inner accomplishment. The student recognized her immediately as the teacher he had been looking for all his life – the one who was going to reveal the answers to the questions on his mind.

That day, he immediately wanted to blurt out his questions and have them answered. He wanted to ask about averting the bombs. However, Khun Yay was on her way to a previous engagement. She just returned his greeting, saying, "Today I've got an appointment I have to go to – we'll have to keep the talk for another day. I've got a funeral to attend."

Even to have heard that much from Khun Yay already raised the student's hopes. He willed tomorrow to come quickly and the very next morning returned to the temple expectantly. He had been looking for an answer to these questions since his childhood, but in vain. He had taken as many opportunities as he could to visit renowned temples to learn their teachings and search out answers — but the ones he received failed to satisfy him. Khun Yay answered these questions so clearly that day he was convinced to study and practice Dhamma with her.

Later on, after term started the student came to meditate with her every day. It was quite a long journey for him to travel from Kasetsart University, crossing the Chao Phaya River to Wat Paknam

Bhasicharoen. It took almost an hour-and-a-half to reach the destination. He would leave the university in the morning, go to meditate with Khun Yay and return to the university again in the evening. Usually he would arrive in the early afternoon and return late in the day.

This student was the first to refer to Teacher Chandra as 'Khun Yay', later on, others changed to call her that too. On their first meeting, Khun Yay didn't waste much time with pleasantries but had her student sit for meditation, teaching him the method. She told him, "Make sure you sit for meditation frequently." He took the meditation seriously and did as he had been told. He was half-surprised at himself for taking Khun Yay's advice so seriously. He didn't have the doubts in his mind which he always had to struggle with when visiting other schools of meditation. He didn't feel Khun Yay had to justify the things she asked him to do. He felt happy just to comply.

It was New Year's Eve. There were many parties and festivities going on for students at Kasetsart University. As he had no secrets from Khun Yay, even behind her back, he went to ask her permission first before going to the party. Khun Yay didn't stop him, she just said, "You go to the party every year and this year you can go *too* – I won't stop you – but don't go into the party before midnight." Accordingly, he conversed with Khun Yay on Dhamma subjects until about 8 p.m. He arrived on campus and had something to eat just outside until 10 p.m.. He knew perfectly well that if he waited until midnight, all the entertainment would be finished, but he wouldn't go back on his word. He walked past all the celebrations without even looking up. He hung around the cattle pen of the university looking again and again at his wrist-watch until the hands reached midnight — then he jumped up like a jack-in-a-box and rushed to the celebrations just in time to see everyone getting on their bikes to go home.

This was just one of many examples of how Khun Yay tested him to see if he really was earnest about his Dhamma studies. In spite of everything, he kept up his practice. Maybe it was because of something Khun Yay had said to him the first time they had had time to talk in earnest. Khun Yay had divulged that, "You're the one the Great Abbot had me summon down to be born during the Second World War."

When he was visiting Wat Paknam at the week-end he would sit for meditation morning, noon and night. If visitors came, he would secrete himself in the temple cloisters and would return to Khun Yay *kuti* when they had gone home. He'd sit leaning his back against the 'headless' pillar. Most of Khun Yay's students before him had been passed down to her from Khun Yay Thongsuk after her death. Although he wasn't her first student, because of his earnest he soon overtook many who had come before him.

Khun Yay made a lot of time for this earnest student. Apart from teaching him the way to meditate until being able to attain the Dhammakåya for himself, she would take the trouble to answer any questions he had for her, even if they didn't seem very important ones.

When the student first met Khun Yay, she still used to chew betel nut. However, when the student kept asking her about 'why' she chose to chew it and 'what' the benefits of betel were, 'whether' it tasted good, Khun Yay merely said it was 'relaxing' to do so. She said some mouthfuls tasted good, others not. She would spit out the betel which tasted *less* appetizing. Eventually she got fed up with the questioning and one day she just quit what had been the habit of a lifetime.

In the beginning, when the student started to study the knowledge of *Dhammakāya* for himself, Khun Yay would always be there to give him encouragement — something he never received even from his own parents. She passed on a recipe for success to him – saying that he should strive continuously, while making sure that his technique was correct. He had to meditate every day without exception. Even if he was so tired that he fell asleep sometimes as he meditated, he should still meditate anyway. He should be observant of whether he had kept to the technique Khun Yay had stipulated.

Normally Khun Yay was active and of strong of health. Although she looked underweight, she shone with happiness and radiance. Once though, when she was taken ill, she was allowed to convalesce at a place in Sukumvit Road, which at that time was still mostly open fields. Her student decided to visit her there, not only to pay a sick visit, but to continue learning from her. By the time he managed to walk to the house on Sukhumvit, he was soaked with perspiration. It was several kilometres he had walked. Inside the house, he saw Khun Yay flat out on her sick bed. Even as she lay there, she explained that he had to do 'this' or 'that' in his meditation. She kept teaching even though not strong enough to sit up in bed. She treated her illness as if it were someone else's. Her student, also disinterested in her illness sat in meditation at the side of her bed, trying his best to put into practice everything she was teaching him, the perspiration hardly dry yet from his journey. These were some of the happiest years of his studentship with Khun Yay.

When she had recovered, the student came for meditation with Khun Yay at Wat Paknam every day. He felt that he learned something new from her every day and wanted to progress in his meditation with her continuously. There was nothing more in the world he would rather do than this.

Once this young meditator raised the question to his teacher, Khun Yay, about a very ancient ceremony for the offering of sustenance to the Buddha — whether it was practical to perform this offering through the practice of *Dhammakāya* meditation. Khun Yay confirmed that it could be done and the young the student learned in detail, the way of offering food to the Buddhas. This offering became more and more popular as it attracted the attention of many others. The ancient sacred rituals of the Thais thereby became better understood and accepted by that generation of meditators.

He was diligent in his practice and became an outstanding student. Consequently, he started to introduce some of his university friends, both male and female, senior and junior, to practice meditation at Khun Yay's place.

In addition, from 1964 onwards, Khun Yay and the student started to meditate with the resolve that all like minded pursuers of perfection join the Dhammaprasit group, to help shoulder the work of spreading the Knowledge of *Dhammakāya* far and wide.

Soon, many more young students showed up at Dhammaprasit House. The ceremony for offering sustenance was taken very seriously and was attended by more and more young students. On the first Sunday of each month, this ceremony was performed by the whole congregation of Dhammaprasit House guided by Khun Yay for the blessing of all people on Earth. Dhammaprasit House became virtually full of people of all ages and all walks of life.

The group was fascinated by the unassuming, humble life of Khun Yay. The hut was small, but every square inch of it was spotlessly clean. Young students lingered behind after the offering of food to the Buddha on Sunday and Khun Yay spent many hours, on many days explaining to them the virtues of practising Buddhism and leading a life of celibacy. This was a real inspiration for all of them. She was able to give straight-forward answers to all the questions they raised.

In 1966 the student was introduced to Khun Phadet Pongsawat who at that time wore a plaid lumberjack shirt and jeans and had an intimidating disposition, a voice loud enough to stop a stampeding buffalo herd in its tracks and the build of a boxer. He had the personal motto 'the thoroughbred never gets fat'.

Khun Phadet was three years the student's senior at Kasetsart. He had just arrived back from two years of placement in Australia. The two met at the university's Loy Kratong party on 27 November. Such a party was held only once every four years. On first sight, despite great differences of character, the two got along like a house on fire – because despite the intimidating first impression Phadet gave, he was enthusiastic to understand Buddhism, but in his pursuit of knowledge had become caught up in black magic. He offered the student a drink – which normally would have been more a *command* than an invitation coming from a senior to a junior. To his surprise, the student said, "I don't drink alcohol. I'm keeping the Precepts." The word 'Precepts' seemed to awaken something in Khun Phadet's heart which was to restore him to the path of the Dhamma from that day forth.

Khun Yay's approach to training up meditators was to start by training up someone who could be an example to the rest. Amongst her male students the person who fitted the bill as an exemplar was the young student Chaiyaboon. This student became the standard which other protégés of hers like Khun Phadet had to meet. Amongst the women, Khun Khaengkhae Jirachutroj was taken as an exemplar and mentor for the younger *female* students. Khun Yay would be very strict in making sure the groups of male and female student didn't become a distraction for one another.

She would say, "If there's one thing I hate, it is messing about between those of the same Dhamma community!"[1] She precluded possible problems, when the meditation class finished at 8 p.m. by having Khun

---

1.*wong boon diaw gan*

Khaengkhae leave to go home first, taking with her all the female students. Only, ten to twenty minutes later, once the ladies were all safely on the bus home, would she allow the gentlemen to take their leave. Only if the gentlemen had urgent business were their group allowed to return first, and the ladies would be kept back for ten to twenty minutes until the *gentlemen* were safely on the bus home. These are the strict precautions Khun Yay took so that her young students would have the full opportunity to benefit from her Dhamma teachings. No scandals or superstitions were ever to undermine the unity of the pioneer working group of Dhammaprasit House.

She would always say to her students:

> "Don't keep secrets from me. If you have prob-
> lems then tell me about them – so that I can
> help. Regard me as you would a parent. Your
> parents can however only understand things
> that will benefit you in present lifetime. I look
> at things that will benefit you in future lifetimes
> too. I feel responsible for you even in lifetimes
> to come. I'm afraid that if you do some things,
> you'll end up in hell after your death. We'll
> have no chance to meet up any more. You'll
> miss your chance to meet up with the Great
> Abbot of Wat Paknam. You'll not have access
> to the knowledge of *Dhammakāya* any more.
> These are the sort of things that worry me – so
> don't keep things secret from me."

Thus from that day onwards, her students didn't keep anything back from Khun Yay any more. If they'd done something wrong, they'd tell her, so that she could advise them of the harm that would come if they continued such behaviours. She wouldn't talk merely of the harm in the present lifetime, but harm in future lifetimes as well. She would nurture her students allowing them to grow on the path of the Dhamma and master their chastity.

This was how Khun Yay formed up her team – the starting point of a group respecting purity above all, who were to be the seed of spreading the Dhamma-kaaya Tradition around the world – arrangements behind the scenes which influenced young people, who would usually be interested in nothing more than starting their own families, inspiring them instead to sacrifice themselves for the prosperity of Buddhism. It was to take her ten years to train up this group to her satisfaction – a team who could co-operate on any task without internal conflicts.

The purity of the lifestyle Khun Yay trained them in was in keeping with the Buddha's own definition of the word 'pure'. 'Clean in body' meant to be moral in bodily action, refraining from killing, stealing and adultery. 'Cleanliness of speech' meant to refrain from telling lies, divisive speech, swearing and idle chatter. 'Cleanliness of mind' meant to be free of the intentions of greed for others' possessions, from vengefulness and being of Right View.[1] Only in these ways can a person truly be considered 'clean'.

Khun Yay Acharn was an exemplar of cleanliness on all levels both inner and outer. She was a person who had loved cleanliness since childhood. She explained we cannot have an uncluttered mind if we live in an untidy environment. An example of her cleanliness is that when she cleaned a chair she did it thoroughly,

---

1. An outlook on the world that alerts and motivates one towards self-improvement.

from front to back, from left to right, from the top to bottom, not missing even the underside. All religious property had to be kept clean all day. She especially emphasised cleanliness in the kitchen and the toilet because if the most unclean and untidy places could be kept clean then everywhere could be kept clean.

The way Khun Yay dressed was unlike anyone else. Her clothes, although simple or worn, were always spotless. Although her nun's robes were often patched or worn, but they were never creased or dirty. Khun Phadet once asked her, "How come your blouse is worn, but it's cleaner than my own shirt which is almost new?" Khun Yay explained:

> "I'm just a farmer's daughter. I don't have many sets of clothes, so I have to do my laundry every day. The dirt on the clothes doesn't have long enough to get engrained because it's already laundered and on the washing line. Once dry, I'm quick to take it off the line and put it away."

Before then Khun Phadet admitted he'd never thought to wash rags and re-use them. He'd always thrown them away when they were dirty. Khun Yay would keep everything clean enough to wear, down to the rags for mopping the floor!

Once in the evening when Khun Yay had led the students in meditation for about ten minutes, she let them continue in silence and disappeared into the toilets. Khun Phadet noticed that after the meditation, the toilet was cleaner than it had been before and curiosity led him to follow her next time she disappeared during a meditation session. He found her cleaning and polishing the toilet bowl and wiping the floor of the toilet until it was completely dry. No matter how the toilet had been left before her, she always left the toilet looking for the next person as if they were the *first* to use it. Part of Khun Yay's motivation for being so careful about the cleanliness of the toilet was the risk of slipping over on a wet floor for a person of advancing years.

Having set an example by her own practice, she wished that her own students follow in her footsteps by freeing themselves of worry and household commitments – so that they could devote themselves to pursuing the Perfections. Thus amongst students of hers who were still single she encouraged celibacy. In the evenings as she was teaching meditation, she would insert encouragement for her students to keep a life of celibacy. In fact, what she taught was always connected with wholesome behaviours, pursuit of perfection, this lifetime and the next. Khun Yay would often praise those who stayed single – saying that it was free like being like a little bird in the sky with nothing to worry about but its own wings and tail. If one doesn't get mixed up in a relationship or start a family, then one too is as free as a bird. She said:

> "if you live alone with one-hundred Baht you can use all of it as you please. The moment you have a family though, you can only consider donating fifty Baht of it at the most. Once you have your first child, you can only consider donating twenty-five Baht. If you have a second child, you might only be able to donate twelve and a half Baht. If you have three or more children, you hardly have the ability to donate anything to Buddhism.

Children look cute enough when they're small, but it's difficult to know how stubborn they'll be when they're older. This is why it's more convenient not to get mixed up in a relationship in the first place. One can pursue perfection without having to be worried about anyone else."

It was a life of freedom – with a minimum of worries and no need to spend time currying favour with others, allowing one to use the limited time available to cultivate one's mind and maintain one's purity of mind. When one's mind is free of the hooks of external people or objects, it is better able to slip inwards towards inner experience. This is how Khun Yay managed to devote all her waking hours to practising the Dhamma throughout her life. Although she sometimes came across those who either didn't understand her intentions or flattered her for them, she was unmoved by them because her mind was already firmly established inside.

Birthdays were always a popular celebration and Khun Yay's birthday was no exception. Her students would organize a celebration on the anniversary according to the lunar calendar.[1] In 1968 her birthday coincided with the tenth of January. After about 10-15 of the students meditated with Khun Yay, spruced up her *kuti* and heard a Dhamma talk by her. She taught them:

"I love all of you like my own children. All of you are so virtuous, strive in your meditation and do everything in earnest. Your meditation is progressing — but, you know, I'd love you even more if you gave up smoking!"

_____
1. the tenth day of the waxing moon of the second lunar month.

97

Khun Yay's word had a certain power to them — because no sooner had she spoken them, all the assembled students, including Khun Phadet, discarded the remainder of their cigarettes into Khun Yay's spittoon an made a vow in her presence that they would never smoke again for the rest of their lives — possibly the best birthday present they had to give. That day when everyone had gone home except Khun Chaiyaboon, he gave Khun Yay a present to exceed that which had come before — which was to take a vow before her that he would maintain celibacy for the rest of his life. Khun Yay listened out his oath with great joy and pride in her student. His example inspired many of his friends later to do the same — and Khun Yay's birthday each year became an occasion when her students would set their spiritual ambitions into words, closer and closer to the ideals she inspired.

The student group were all young, enthusiastic people, firm believers in the doctrine of the Buddha. With great ambition, they were devout Buddhists and ready to spread the Teaching of the Buddhas to the world. The group seemed to grow larger and larger each day. As the group grew, Khun Yay maintained the original determination and virtue of the pioneer students. She always taught her students to remain chaste, reminding them of the burdensome nature of the householder's life. Indeed her student often wanted to drop out from his studies at Kasetsart — so strong was his sense of urgency to ordain. However, Khun Yay would not let him, saying she would only permit him to ordain if he had already graduated. He would have to be a scholar both of worldly and spiritual knowledge and bring both of these to bear for the prosperity of Buddhism. Because of the poverty of her own educational background, she was always very supportive of educational initiatives of all kinds in just the way the Great Abbot had been. He had always inspired people to study hard even though he knew that the supreme goal in life comes through meditation.

A short time later, the student graduated and soon afterwards on the twenty-seventh of August 1969 — the full-moon day of the ninth month in the Thai lunar calendar — members of the Dhammaprasit group gathered inside the Shrine Hall of Wat Paknam, as the student entered into the monkhood, accomplishing his intention for his life's dedication to Buddhism as 'Ven. Dhammajayo Bhikkhu'.

He had a full understanding of the reality of life — that things are not permanent — that man and all creatures are destined to die and there is no true certainty in anything. Seeking for the real Truth is the utmost goal for all creatures. Ven. Dhammajayo made a solemn vow to himself, to fulfil his mission at any cost, any degree of self-sacrifice, to bring all creatures to attain the highest bliss of Nirvana. This ordination was a great milestone for Dhammaprasit House which now had in its midst, a very talented meditation teacher. At that time, Khun Yay was already sixty-one years old. At that time, the number of people coming for meditation at Dhammaprasit House was so many that for the major ceremonies, they overfilled both the house itself, its balconies and the lawn in front of the house. There was literally 'standing room only' for the ceremony for offering sustenance to the Lord Buddha held each first Sunday of the month. Since the number of students at Dhammaprasit started to exceed the space available to her, she started to entertain the idea of building a new temple from scratch. Khun Yay planned everything for the building of the temple. This had been her intention for a long time but she had been waiting for her successor to ordain first. Once ordained, the new monk would need to have his own place to use as a school of meditation – so there would need to be a temple where people could come to learn meditation. They aspired to spread of Buddhism to foreign countries, the growth of Dhammakåya meditation bringing peace to all countries in the world. It seemed very certain that Dhammaprasit House could no longer fulfil the strong and virtuous ambitions of the members if they were to complete their mission. It was about this time that Khun Yay knew it was the right time to start building a temple of her own.

11
Establishing Dhammakaya Temple

Sayaṃ āyavayaṃ jaññā   sayaṃ jaññā katākataṃ
Nigganhe niggahārahaṃ   pagganhe paggahārahaṃ

The leader must be aware of expenditure and income themselves, of what work has been completed or which remains to be done. They must criticise those worthy of criticism and praise those worthy of praise.

J.v.116

Khun Yay was looking for a twenty-acre plot of land to build a temple. One day, as Ven. Dhammajayo was meditating, he saw a vast expanse of paddy field close to the bank of a canal. He was able to recognise the location of the land as being in Pathumthani province, and he found out that it belonged to a very old landowner who would be virtuous enough to consider parting with the land for the purposes of the Dhammaprasit group. Khun Yay delegated Khun Thawin Watti-rangkul (then not yet ordained as a nun) to go and negotiate with the owner, Lady Prayat Paetyapongsa-visudhathibodee to see if they would let the Dhammaprasit meditation group buy the plot.

Quite by coincidence, when they met this old lady it was her birthday — a day when she was intending to do the biggest merit of her life. When they said they wanted to purchase about twenty acres of land for the sake of building a Buddhist temple, this lady was overwhelmed and refused to sell *any* part of her land. She would not rent it to them either. She said that she would instead *give* them the whole of this land, four times more than they had asked — and this was to be the start of the Dhamma Practice Centre.[1]

Subsequently, Ven. Dhammajayo asked Khun Yay about the feasibility of a temple where hundreds of people would come and hundreds of monks would stay. Khun Yay asked Khun Phadet the amount of money that would be necessary to set up that sort of temple. Khun Phadet replied that it would be around 100 million Baht. Khun Yay meditated and came back with a confident grin saying that whether the number coming to the temple were in the hundreds or the thousands, out of her great compassion she would be able to provide for all of them.

Khun Yay then proudly brought out the brown envelope she had been using for collecting donations. This was the money they were going to use to build the temple. They counted it and found there was only 3,200 Baht (~USD$80). Khun Phadet asked her, "How can we build a temple with only 3,200 Baht?" Khun Yay asked him, "If you received a budget of 100 million Baht from the government for training people to be virtuous and to devote their lives for Buddhism like you and the team; how many people would you get?" Khun Phadet replied that one could not be certain of training even a single good person — even if one had a hundred million Baht. Khun Yay told him with a grin that

---

1.*Soon putthajak patipat thamm*

she already had *eleven* virtuous and devoted people, which was worth much *more* than a hundred million Baht and was certain they would succeed.

At the time when she started out with the temple, there were very few volunteers to help her — but they were all those she had trained up herself, from the time they were still students. And those students were very exceptional, because normally in teenage, no-one thinks to lead a life of celibacy. Normally teenagers just think 'how young and beautiful I am', 'how handsome', 'how healthy I am', 'I should go and have fun while I'm in the prime of life' — but this group, who Khun Yay trained up became more and more interested in meditation and wanted to keep the Eight Precepts[1] for the rest of their lives, and for the gentlemen, many wanted to take lifelong ordination too. Thus, there were about ten monks or volunteers in the temple, helping Khun Yay to build the temple.

As seen from the old pictures, the temple was no more than barren land. These people were so faithful in Buddhism that they thought nothing was beyond them. They would find a way to bring success to the temple. This is why Khun Yay said she was a multi-millionaire. She was not a millionaire in terms of western economic values, but in terms of Buddhist economic values — where it's not just about figures, where even faith and goodwill are counted as assets.

It was about that time that Khun Yay's disciples compiled a book by the name *Walking Towards Happiness*[2] in order to reach out to those who might help them

---

1.Stricter version of the Five Precepts which upgrades the third Precept to refrain from uncelibacy and adds not eating after midday, refraining from immodesty amd refraining from indulgence in sleeping.

2. *Duen bai su kwam suk*

to build the new temple. The book brought together the testimonies and experiences of various eminent disciples of the Dhammakāya Tradition telling the reason why the temple had to be built. Khun Yay couldn't write down her own story to go in the book, so she told her story to others who wrote it down for her. It turned out to be a book which inspired many of its readers to come forth and help with the work of building the temple.

The Dhammaprasit group headed by Khun Yay began establishing the temple after making the vow:

> "We will devote all our flesh and blood, body and mind, intelligence and wealth in homage to the Lord Buddha in order to set up a meditation centre following the Way of *Dhammakāya*."

The temple was established with a ground-breaking ceremony on Māgha Pūjā Day, the twentieth of February 1970.

Before starting on the work of building the temple, Khun Yay called a meeting of everyone involved in order to avert any problems likely to crop up in their work. She said that although the temple was large and would take a long time to complete, she insisted that it be built to the highest standards.

She predicted that personal conflict would be sure to rear its ugly head as they worked together on the temple and that anyone who knew themselves to be easily provoked by conflict could remove themselves immediately to the back of the crowd. However, anyone who *could* work in a conflict situation without being annoyed could come to sit close by her. The situation needed a lot of patience and

Khun Yay used to use the motto, "We may disagree, but we must never be opposed" (i.e. everyone can voice their opinion, can discuss their views, but this must never lead to deadlock). This meant that however many people there were, they would be unified in their quest to attain the Triple Jewel, the *Dhammakāya* inside. Khun Phadet, was thus put in charge of looking after the eighty acre plot and to oversee all the construction work to take place on the land too.

Once Khun Phadet saw Khun Yay making a very extended resolution and asked what was so important for her to make a wish at such length. Khun Yay replied that she was making the wish that she might never be responsible for taking life, in any future lifetime, not even so much as the life of a humble ant or termite — and equally the wish that no living being may ever be responsible for killing her — even if she should be alone faced with an entire army of aggressors in the same way that the Buddha had been confronted with Māra's army on the night of his enlightenment. Khun Phadet had the impression that Khun Yay wanted to teach him a personal lesson, because at that time the temple was being threatened by those who wanted to burn down the thatch-roofed lecture hall used at the time. Deep in Phadet's mind, there was the temptation to finish off those troublemakers once and for all — but faced with the earnestness of Khun Yay's resolve warning him of the danger of even a misplaced intention, it took all the wind out of the sails of his aggression.

The establishment of the temple had three components: the plan of work, the plan for personnel and the financial plan. At the time of establishing the temple, the whole of the plan of work was already in the heart of Ven. Dhammajayo, the Abbot. However, the financial plan and the plan for personnel were still undeveloped. There was only the plan of work — the plan for personnel and finances were to come hand-in-hand later on.

However inestimable the amount of resources and money is needed, it was obvious that the transcending factor was the quality of the personnel needed to make Wat Phra Dhammakāya a success. In the words of the Abbot:

> "the people who perform this work must for sure be loving, with devotion and self-sacrifice to the extent that they are prepared to put their lives on the line."

To make the plan of work manifest, the abbot started to build the temple with his own two hands and the determination to build the ideal place for meditation and Dhamma practice. He prayed that when people came to see the driving force of virtue in the temple, that they too would be inspired to give a helping hand with the abbot's scheme. In the beginning, the temple was just eighty acres of paddy field open to the sky. There were no trees to give shade because the soil was virtually infertile. The abbot needed to create an environment suitable for meditation. Trees were needed to shade the place and a network of canals was designed to make the temple cool and suitable for meditation.

At that stage the temple didn't have a lot of money. Furthermore, the number of people always seemed to outstrip the resources available to give support.

When the land was transferred to them, Khun Yay invited the entire Dhammaprasit group to see the place for the first time – because many had contributed funds to buy the land without ever having seen it. When they caught sight of the plot of land which was barren paddy fields across the whole of its extent as far as the eye could see, many couldn't imagine how it could ever be transformed into a huge temple.

The level of the land in the paddy fields was three metres lower than it needed to be. Thus the pioneers needed to dig out the canal bed and to raise the level of the ground as 'islands' above the level of the water in the paddy-fields. The islands needed to be at least six metres wide and needed containment piles to give them the required shape. A dredger with volunteers from the Irrigation Ministry was used for this work. It would dig down for three-and-a-half metres and the soil dredged would be heaped-up to form new islands. The canals already in existence needed to be filled in.

Having dug out the canals in the eighty-acre area, Ven. Dhammajayo invited all the supporters of Dhammaprasit House to take a tour round the eighty acre site in the Irrigation Ministry barge. Once the supporters saw the plans of the temple falling into place, everyone got together to contribute the funds necessary for building the first *kuti*s on the site.

At the time when the temple was being established, Khun Yay wasn't yet resident there. However, when she visited, her daily routine at the temple would be quite regular. She would rise at about 3.00 a.m. to sit for meditation to facilitate the arrival of donations and volunteers needed for the temple construction to be fulfilled. After breakfast, she would sit for meditation until about 11.00H.. After taking her own lunch, she would be seen preparing a bucket, a machete and a hoe and would invite the temple laypeople to help plant out trees. However, many generations of trees were lost because the soil at the temple was very acid [pH = 4]. Not many species could tolerate that degree of acidity, but it turned out that the one which *could* survive was wattle [*Acacia auriculaeformis Cunn.*]. It was a pioneer species and its nitrifying properties had the ability to transform the consistency of the soil. Wattle was the only survivor when all the other trees had died but under the influence of this tree, the soil improved sufficiently in quality to allow other species to be planted too, especially eucalyptus.

As the soil quality improved, she planted an incredible variety of tree species whether it be *Annonaceae* shrubs, *Mimusops*, Rose Chestnut, ilang-ilang, *Apocynaceae* or *Pterocarpus*. The trees seen today are the few survivors. Trees had been planted and replaced over and over again. Some were buried during constructions of buildings and infrastructures. But Khun Yay never gave up, she kept trying new species until she found survivors. She was happy all the trees could make a safe home for wild birds. Khun Yay had a fondness for trees. However, with so many chickens and peacocks which had been released in the temple, she wouldn't trust anyone to leave saplings at ground level, but instead constructed a hammock where the saplings could be stored out of reach until they could be planted out. If useful trees bore seeds, she told her attendants to keep them for her to germinate.

Sometimes in order to plant a tree, they had to level the soil first. Often her helpers ploughed up trees she had planted previously, but she never had a word of complaint. She just enjoyed herself planting trees, even though at that time she was over sixty. Often the young men helping her gave up *before* her out of exhaustion. She worked unflaggingly throughout the shadeless heat of the day. At one stage she became so physically weak from her labours that she didn't even have the strength to rise from her bed — let alone walk. Fearing that she would die, her followers called a doctor from Chulalongkorn University who diagnosed her condition as undernourishment! She would keep on planting trees until four or five in the evening. Only then would she take a wash and prepare for evening chanting at 8.00 p.m.. Meditation would finish at nine or ten p.m. and they would go to rest. This was her daily routine throughout the period of construction of the temple.

Every Friday, Luang Phaw Dhammajayo would make time to prepare for giving a sermon and leading meditation on the upcoming Sunday. He wouldn't accept invitations anywhere else on the Saturday. He would merely receive guests if there were any and would sit in meditation for the whole of the rest of the day. Meanwhile on Friday, all the rest of the monks in the temple including Khun Phadet would lead volunteers who had come for the weekend, in meditation – before they helped Khun Yay with the planting out of trees.

In the beginning, life at the new temple was full of hardship. There was hardly any drinking water because all the soil in the area was highly acidic. To render the groundwater potable, they had to dose it with alum to precipitate out the toxins, boil it and carefully pour off the drinkable part leaving a thick scum at the bottom of the pot. However, such difficulties failed to discourage the pioneers who were more intent on the meritorious task of constructing the new temple.

At that time there were three monks, four or five resident laymen [*upāsaka*] and seven or eight hired workers. The laymen at that time lived at the 'Green House' on the present day site of 'Tāvatiṃsa' and the 'Thai House' which at that time was on the present day site of 'Catumahārājika' Hall. There was also a small kitchen on the site of the present day Yāmā kitchen, but like all the other buildings of that time, it was a temporary structure.

Sometimes funds were short. Khun Phadet would ask Khun Yay, "Do we have a little money left?"

"Yes. There's about a thousand baht left ($25)."

He looked concerned, but Khun Yay looked unruffled as always. "Go and sit for meditation," she advised, "and I'll do the necessary."

Khun Phadet followed her advice and Khun Yay too, sat for a long meditation from six until nine p.m.. After the meditation, Khun Phadet admitted to Khun Yay, "If I don't have 10,000 to pay the workmen by tomorrow, we're sure to have trouble on our hands."

Khun Yay looked back at him, unruffled as always and maintained, "The necessary funds ought to be arriving by nightfall." Khun Yay looked confident, but Khun Phadet didn't know what more to say – so he bade her goodnight, saying he'd be back early next morning for the wages. As he opened the door to leave, he found man sitting on the stairs outside. On further enquiry, the man said his father had commanded on his deathbed that a donation of 30,000 be brought to this place. He'd been waiting there since 7 p.m. but couldn't enter the house because all the doors were closed and the people inside had gone for meditation!

In the beginning, work at the temple went on all day and all night. Sometimes, because of weariness, there were quarrels amongst the workers. Khun Yay didn't attend the work meetings herself, but she would always be around, in the aisles, keenly observing the community as a whole. When she saw that the community couldn't settle a disagreement she would call the meeting to a close saying, "The meeting will probably drag on much longer – come and meditate with me instead. After a couple of hours of meditation, everyone's quality of mind would be elevated. Only then would she let them continue with the meeting. This time the meeting would always go much more smoothly. These are the management skills demonstrated by Khun Yay in spite of her lack of education. Whether it be management of people, places or assets, Khun Yay would show moderation in all things. Everything she did lacked excess. Unity arose naturally as a by-product of her presence.

In early 1970 Khun Phadet decisively took his lifelong vow of celibacy even though he could not yet ordain, still with a lot more construction work to oversee. Nevertheless, Khun Yay had advised him to take this vow because he *had* previously considered marriage, but had been brought to his senses by his father who chided him, "If you want to marry do so,

111

but answer me within the next seven days what virtues you think you have to pass on to your prospective wife and children." Khun Yay had driven it home to him with the advice:

> "Phadet! You'll never make a go of it in the lay life because you're too kind-hearted. You'll feel sorry for people and give away everything you own. If you have a family relying on you, then you'll all face hardship. You were born to pursue perfection – not for any other path in life. If you ordain, that is your pathway to fulfilment in life. You have the potential to see and know the reality of all that is in the Buddhist Scriptures."

In time, Luang Phaw Dattajeevo was to ordain on 19 December 1971. Everything went well for him except that he had to exercise special self-control not to continue using the gestures of respect for Khun Yay he had used all along as a layman. Now he was a monk, with more Precepts than Khun Yay as a nun, it was no longer right for him to put his hands in a gesture of respect to her, even if he thought she deserved it. Khun Yay knew his difficulty and brought him to his senses with the words, "Don't do that – otherwise the demerit will be mine!"

In 1973, the new temple was ready for the Working Group to move from its former base in Dhammaprasit House. Ven. Dattajeevo was in his second year of monkhood. The amenities in the temple provided almost all the necessary conveniences for accommodation. Khun Yay would attend to these monks needs by regularly sending Phra Kru Palad Wanchai Sīlavaṇṇo (at that time not yet ordained) with a carload of provisions from Wat Paknam. Khun Yay ordered that banana trees be planted all around the Ven. Dattajeevo's *kuti*, much to the Venerable's surprise:

"What are all these banana trees for? Surely they're not for me to eat?" he asked Khun Yay.

As if she knew him all to well, she replied, "They're for you to kick! If you ever get annoyed, you can kick them down instead of kicking the people who may cause you irritation. You can't go kicking people any more, because now you're a monk."

From that day forward, even the sight of a banana tree would make him laugh, thinking of Khun Yay's advice – who knew him all to well for his previous quick temper.

Once the fundamental amenities of the temple had been completed, Ven. Dhammajayo expressed his wish to give Dhamma training courses in both theory and practice, for the benefit of young people and the general public, in order to elevate their quality of mind and forge virtue in society. This was part of his master plan for building up a foundation of personnel for the temple. In fact, the idea was an extrapolation of Khun Yay's approach to training which she had passed on to him when he first ordained.

As a way to propagate and strengthen the religion, the abbot, Ven. Dhammajayo set out to nurture the children and adults coming to the temple into truly learned people. This meant making them learned both in the ways of the world and in the ways of Dhamma. The abbot recognised the importance of this link between the two fields of knowledge coining the motto, "Knowledge must go hand-in-hand with virtue". The biochemist who uses his skills to refine heroin or the farmer who grows opium in the place of food crops, are examples of those learned in the world but who do not see the importance of virtue. The abbot set out to create a training which would instil virtue in the hearts of students, at a time before they took up their worldly vocation, so that virtue would be the basis of these young peoples' service to society.

The 'Heirs of the Dhamma' [*Dhammadāyāda*] Training Scheme was organised for this purpose for the first time in 1972. The Dhammadāyāda Training had been announced around the universities as a 'Summer Course in Meditation Training'. It was the first major project of the temple and from that time onwards became an annual fixture.

The first course consisted of two groups, with a total attendance of sixty. Male students, they were all provided with a white suit of rough cotton, printed with the Dhammadāyāda logo. At that time, the temple still had no significant shade from trees, so the 'ascetic practice umbrellas' [*klod*], under which they slept, were completely exposed to the midday heat, where they had been pitched. The course was lead by the Vice-Abbot, Ven. Dattajeevo himself, who stayed in a '*klod*' alongside the trainees. The trainees underwent a rigorous two-week course of training under the Vice-Abbot's direction, rising at 3.45 a.m., following Eight Precepts and spending a full twelve hours-a-day in sitting meditation. Many of the trainees were very successful in their meditation as a result of this training and many of those pioneering 'heirs of Dhamma' were to go on to become the elder monks of the temple in the present day.

Many, many people underwent the 'Dhammadāyāda' training course because of the reputation for the training in *Dhammakāya*. It was this training which lead so many of the young students to become members of the temple. The innocence of youth, through this training was to become the pride and confidence of the temple. These people gained the capability to be leaders of the religion.

The abbot looked for graduates with a Batchelors' degree for whom meditation was the keystone in life. Because the basic standards for personnel were high, when the numbers interested started to increase, those with faith and money to support the temple followed too. Young students gave their support to the temple too. This was the start of the Buddhist societies and Buddhist study societies in the universities and colleges. The Buddhist societies were to integrate Buddhism into education of young people in Thailand through their various projects. This was the kingpin in the plan for training the personnel of the temple. When the number of personnel started to increase, the level of faith increased and the level of support for the temple started to grow.

Just as in the beginning, it was the enthusiasm of the young people which led to the growth of the temple, it has been young people in the present day who recognise the importance of the search for knowledge and the correct way of putting the knowledge into practice, using the Buddha's Teaching as the key. In regard to young people's usual attitude to their own conduct, the Dhammadāyāda course has been the turning-point in the thinking and point-of-view of Thailand's Youth. It has lead more than ten-thousand young people, over nearly twenty years to leave the bright and coloured lights of modern youth for self-training in the Buddha's Teaching. It has lead many wayward students to get down to their studies and to become the admiration of their parents.

Khun Yay explained that in forging virtue in peoples' hearts it is necessary to instil them with the qualities of a Wise One [*paṇḍita*] – those who are wise both in worldly and spiritual ways. All those who wish true happiness in life must be educated in virtue hand in hand with their worldly knowledge. Khun Yay had also expressed the wish that trainees would become an important force in helping to spread the Dhamma as a result of their training.

By 1975 most of the important amenities in the temple were almost complete – whether it be the pavilion for meditation practice, *kuti*s for monastic accommodation. In about April, Khun Yay and Luang Phaw Dhammajayo moved permanently to the temple from Wat Paknam.

Khun Yay was the one to lay down many of the ground rules for the temple. She kept a watchful eye over all her students and gave them encouragement. They needed encouragement because building the temple was a challenge – it was only those with a clear vocation in mind who would be able to cope.

Khun Yay reflected on the most important regulations to lay down for the long-term success of the temple, using the example of the Great Abbot of Wat Paknam as her blueprint, saying, "All my monks are young and inexperienced." Thus she laid down the ground rules as follows:

1. The temple gate should be locked at six p.m. and opened at six a.m.
2. Monks are strictly prohibited from receiving guests at their own *kuti*s – especially female guests

Furthermore, she considered that if the number of monks at Wat Phra Dhammakåya were to increase, almsfood would be insufficient for the monks and certainly insufficient for the congregation members attending the temple or volunteers helping at the temple. Thus she suggested that Luang Phaw Dhammajayo follow the Great Abbot's example and set up a temple kitchen.

In her nature, Khun Yay had a love of cleanliness, honesty, sincerity and orderliness. There is an unwritten code of conduct which has come down to the temple since the time of Dhammaprasit House. Following these principles has lead to the segregation of the sexes in the temple with separate accomodation for resident laymen, resident laypeople and monks in the temple. Khun Yay has discouraged physical contact between the temple members, even between those of the same gender. She taught that if you are not refined in your outward behaviour, you cannot expect to be refined in the meditation you practice. The polite table manners, the polite manner of speech, neat dress, tidiness and the traditional Thai 'family-like' relations which were the foundation of respect between the temple members, formed a culture in the temple. This culture is a habitual discipline to ensure harmonious community living and was a way of life in which newcomers to the temple had to train themselves upon arrival.

Visitors to the temple were expected to exhibit the same sort of good conduct and attention to detail as the residents and for this reason Khun Yay commissioned a sign displaying the temple's basic rules on the outside wall of the Tāvatiṃsa building, namely: "The Dhammakāya Meditation Centre is a Sanctuary of Virtue for all Buddhists. It is a place which needs to be tranquil, clean, tidy and restrained, in keeping with Buddhist identity. Thus, visitors should help to sustain the Buddhist religion, so that it can prosper, by keeping strictly to the following rules, under the motto, "The wise love to learn and practise rules of discipline":

1. No smoking and prohibition of addictive substances on the premises;
2. No bringing of merchandise onto the premises for the purposes of trading;
3. No promotions or leafleting of any sort;
4. No reading newspapers or other publications which disturb peace of mind;
5. No radios or playing of musical cassettes;
6. No propaganda, electioneering or canvassing. Only true and useful words should be spoken;
7. No dancing, musical performances, shows, lotteries or games of any sort;
8. No courting, petting or fortune-telling;
9. No unauthorised release of animals on the temple grounds;
10. Dress must be polite and modest. No exaggerated gestures of the hands or feet or lying about in the temple grounds, such as are unattractive to see."

Wat Phra Dhammakāya increasingly gained a reputation for its good discipline amongst other monasteries of Thailand.

Although Khun Yay was the one to lay down the regulations for the temple, she was the first to comply with all of them. As the founder of the temple she remained humble. She never referred to herself as Luang Phaw's teacher. If she had the chance to teach others, she would humble herself by saying:

"These days I'm just one of the residents of the temple. I have to follow the same rules and regulations as you. I am answerable to the abbot in all things."

Khun Yay never was 'above the law' because she herself loved discipline. She would always raise her hands in a gesture of prayer when speaking even to the least senior of the monks or novices in the temple – regardless of the fact that she was teacher to both the abbots. When she met congregation members she would always be the first to greet them.[1] Looking down on people or having airs and graces was alien to her character. Having passed all her authority on to Ven. Dhammajayo, she lived out her simple life, following a fixed daily routine.

Khun Yay was definitive in her decision making and was not interested in what others might say about her decisions. She would go ahead with her decisions as long as they didn't contradict monastic discipline [vinaya], virtue [dhamma] and didn't bring her into conflict. She recognized that the world is

---

1. Normally in Thailand it is the custom for younger people to be the first to greet elders.

of the nature to have the vicissitudes of increase and erosion of wealth, increase and erosion of rank, praise and gossip, happiness and suffering – because even the Lord Buddha had to meet up with the unpleasant side of these things. Some even praise those who are out and out gangsters. Thus Khun Yay made her decisions on the basis of what was *best* rather than what would be popular or necessarily convenient. She used to say:

> "All my life I've had a very simple way of deciding what to do. I never do anything to please anyone, unless it is to please the Lord Buddha himself – because the Buddha is blessed with the ability to discern right and wrong, appropriate and inappropriate, wholesomeness and unwholesomeness. Thus I just do according to what the Buddha taught – and if anyone else reprimands me for that, even if it is everybody in town, I remain unmoved by their protests. I do things to please the Buddha alone."

Luang Phaw Dattajeevo asked her, "And doesn't that make people very angry sometimes?"

"Of course it does!"

"And what do you do when they are angry with you?"

"I meditate going through the centre of the centre continuously aligning my *Dhammakāya* with the body of enlightenment of the Lord Buddha in Nirvana."

Thus Khun Yay was never one to be swayed by fashion or public opinion – and this in turn is why her mind was never perturbed from a steadfast standstill. In this way she was able to lead a whole community in the spreading of the Dhammakāya tradition throughout the world in spite of innumerable hindrances. In the face of obstacles she would neither fight nor run away, but continue to do as many virtuous deeds as ever.

There was also quite a lot of preparation for the reception of Sunday's congregation which needed to be done in the eighty acre area of the temple – whether it be setting out rubbish bins or scrubbing the toilets.

In the olden days Khun Yay would demonstrate how to clean the toilets personally. However, for later generations, proper use of the toilets became integrated into the textbook of Buddhist culture taught to all newcomers staying at the temple. Indeed, newcomers continue to be impressed by the cleanliness of the temple's restrooms even down to the present day. Some had never seen such a clean restroom at other public facilities before. It was volunteers' pride to clean the temple's restrooms, which they called "cleaning the celestial mansion [*vimāna*], with her secret that "the deeper you clean into the toilet bowl, the brighter your mind."

The toilets which Khun Yay took the most care of were the 'toilet block of twenty' almost opposite her own *kuti*. She would lead the volunteers herself, teaching them to scrub 'all the way down the U-bend'. Armed with a scotchbrite and washing powder they raced to complete the task. It was rarely the habit of Khun Yay merely to explain how to do something, but when she was training volunteers she would show them *by example* how it should be done. Especially when they saw the tremendous pride with which Khun Yay herself went about this task, they were inspired to *follow* her example. Furthermore, Khun Yay would explain to them that if they did everything to the very best of their ability this lifetime round, next lifetime would go smoothly without having to redo tasks. This would be the positive karmic fruits they would be taking with them to subsequent lifetimes. She always repeated her advice on how to flush the toilet properly, keep the floor dry, and to turn off taps and lights after use.

Khun Yay even went as far as to demonstrate how the restroom should be *used* appropriately. There can be few masters who taught their students in such details. In the bathroom, Khun Yay started "Whatever you do, you need to have good mindfulness in order to do it properly." Khun Yay taught how to flush the toilet without wasting too much water.[1] After her explanation, she showed how to use a small bucket filled with water for flushing the toilet bowl. She added:

> "After you are done, turn off the tap. If you turn it off loosely, the tap will drip. If you turn it off too tightly, the washer will soon perish. Thus, even turning off the tap you need to know moderation."

As she performed her teaching duties, she seemed to enjoy passing on her practices to the next generation.

The word spread that there was a band of university-educated monks building a huge temple in Patumthani. The news spread to the elder monks governing the province and one day they sent an inspector monk to check whether the temple was up to scratch. The inspector used his usual stratagem of checking only the kitchen and the toilets – because as he explained, you can tell everything about a temple by looking to see if these two places are in order. He disclosed from his inspection that he would expect the new temple to prosper!

1. Upcountry toilets in Thailand are flushed by baling water manually from an adjacent bucket with a bowl.

Once in the late afternoon, Luang Phaw Datta-jeevo was passing Khun Yay's *kuti* and noticed her digging fertilizer around the foot of a tree near her *kuti*. Luang Phaw Dattajeevo approached her and stood behind her at a distance. It was a full four or five minutes before Khun Yay turned to greet him. He asked, "Yay! Now you are in your old age, doesn't tending to so many trees wear you out?"

"No! It still doesn't tire me. While I am working I continue to meditate at my centre – so I don't become tired."

"So what were you meditating on as you were working?"

"As I work I observe the centre of the *Dhammakāya* inside and recollect the previous lifetimes of the Buddhas of the past to see how they pursued perfection and use these observations to see my own shortfalls so that I can improve on myself."

Khun Yay was someone to train herself the whole of the time – taking the same standards used by the Lord Buddhas of the past to train *herself*. Only when a person is able to use the Lord Buddha's teachings to teach themselves, will they be able to use those teachings to teach the rest of the world.

In 1981 the temple was consecrated. Until that time it had been referred to as the 'Dhamma Practice centre'. Since consecration, it has been known by its present name, 'Phra **Dhammakāya** Temple' or 'Wat Phra **Dhammakāya**'.

With the consecration of the temple, the number of people attending increased dramatically. The work of the temple, whether it be outreach, personnel training or construction work had to be done hand-in-hand. The community resident at Wat Phra Dhammakāya became gradually larger – whether it be monks, novices or resident laymen or laywomen. Khun Yay would join the major ceremonies held at the temple and at the age of about eighty years old, she seemed to enjoy seeing laypeople from all over the world participating. She would often exclaim:

"I never thought that there would be so many laypeople coming to our temple. When Ven. Dhammajayo was ordained, we expected only twenty acres of temple land. Now even 1,000 acres is full of laypeople."

12
Khun Yay's
Twilight Years

Kosajjaṃ bhayato disvā   viriyārambañca khemato
Āraddhaviriyā hotha   esā buddhānusāsani

One should see the danger in laziness and that striving
is the origin of happiness. One should strive for oneself.
This is the teaching of the Buddha.

Cariyāpiṭaka 36

The small *kuti* which had been completed at the
temple in 1975 for Khun Yay was in the strategic
position of gatehouse, at the entrance of the monks'
residential area. It was also the closest to the kitchen.
A bird's eye view of the eighty-acre site reveals
that Khun Yay's *kuti* was also situated right in the
geometric centre of the temple's original property.
Surrounded by various types of aromatic plants,
the area had its own natural fragrance. Following a
simple square design, the *kuti* was made of concrete
and painted white.

Until the 1990's Khun Yay used this *kuti* exclu-
sively. Later, she only stayed overnight there but
spent the day at the small office across the road. In
Khun Yay's small *kuti,* her spartan bed was next to
the wall. Khun Yay's bed was a stainless steel frame
topped by a thick piece of wood panel. Over the
wood panel was a thin mattress topped by another
white bed sheet. The bed was just high enough to

allow her to place her feet flat on the floor when on the bed. There was just enough space around her bed to walk around. There was no air conditioner in her room. Inside *kuti* there was only dim light from the light over the door. Khun Yay's room was dark and only street-light penetrated through the windows, leaving the room quiet and restful for meditation.

Khun Yay was disciplined in every daily activity. She was careful about everything she used. She was cautious when using tap water and tried to economise as much as she could. Rinsing her face and mouth gently, no water ever splashed wasted around the basin always leaving it clean and shiny.

Khun Yay remained uncommonly diligent and healthy even as a senior citizen. Although she was close to her eighty-third year, she looked so energetic, fresh and enthusiastic. Even when she was tired she wouldn't nap during the day. Khun Yay appreciated silence and tranquillity while meditating. If there was any noise, she would ask what caused it or simply open her eyes.

Normally, Khun Yay tried to do everything herself. She felt she was imposing on others if they had to help her with personal tasks. People could feel thankfulness whenever they served her. She expressed it through her eyes and what she said. Even when served water, she said *"sadhu!"* Normally, Khun Yay was hesitant to bother anyone. When she visited someone's house, she whispered to her main attendant Khun Areepan Treeanusorn. "Are we imposing on them?" Areepan replied "No, they want to make merit with you."

All Khun Yay's belongings were arranged in an orderly fashion, whether large or small. Things were always arranged in neat lines. Even when she walked by a clothesline of rugs, she would take a moment rearranging them in such a way that the rugs' edges were parallel. Everything that Khun Yay used, would be organized and maintained to the best of her ability.

Behind Khun Yay's *kuti*, there was a downpipe draining rainwater into a large earthenware water butt. The water butt was covered with an aluminium lid. The lid was supposed to be flat but because of age it sagged in the middle and a puddle would collect in the dip. Khun Yay would wipe it dry every time she walked by.[1] Khun Yay never overlooked these small matters.

Nevertheless, Khun Yay's penchant for orderliness didn't stop at personal matters. She taught the volunteers to train themselves in self-discipline by not overlooking the importance of having shoes removed at the pavilion steps arranged neatly, to have brooms and brushes put in a rack and even hanging out washing neatly, irrespective of whether it were rags hung out to dry. She once explained to Luang Phaw Dattajeevo that:

> "Our temple still has room for improvement in its tidiness. When the congregations come to our temple, especially on Sundays they should come across the maximum of positive impressions to take back home with them. Most of the monks here are newly ordained and consequently are still training themselves. They don't have much to teach the congregation. However, a good impression can still be made on the congregation if the temple is clean, shaded, luxuriant – without

---

1. Standing water in a hot climate attracts mosquito larvae, algae and other unhygenic things.

127

overlooking small details. Monks can make sure that they are a good example of enthusiasm to meditate. Everything in the temple needs to be well organized, starting from peoples' shoes. If the shoes are in a mess, before long the brooms, rags and rubbish will be too. Such a messy environment is not conducive to meditation, especially for the newcomers. It'll take them an hour before their mind starts to settle down. As soon as they open their eyes and see all the mess, any inner experience they've gained from their meditation will be all too quickly lost. If only everyone can help with these details, their mind will be tranquil throughout their stay at the temple. Their mind will go automatically to the centre of the body. I've already tried it and it worked for me – because that is the nature of the mind. Even though the congregations coming to the temple might not have the chance to hear a sermon, but seeing a tidy temple they will gain ease of mind and an inspiring example which they can take back home with them."

Wat Phra Dhammakāya has prospered down to the present day because Khun Yay and the temple's pioneers saw the value of orderliness – meaning that even newcomers coming to the temple years later could comply with simple things like removing their shoes in an orderly fashion, without feeling embarrassed. There would be a sign identifying the shoe rack, a symbol showing where the shoes should be put and a volunteer available to answer any queries. Once people understood, the rules of the temple didn't need to be written down any more, but become part of the temple culture. Many usually arrogant people have been humbled merely by the sight of a neatly lined-up row of shoes left by a group going for their morning chanting.

Even later in life, her daily routine remained fixed. From four in the morning until six, she would meditate alone. As soon as it was light, she would be busily arranging things in her midst. At 06.30 a.m. her attendant, Khun Areepan would bring breakfast to her *kuti*. After breakfast, Khun Yay put on a white knitted woollen hat and scarf, warm socks and shoes and would go out on her inspection of the temple. An attendant would ride a tri-shaw to the temple's small office to pick Khun Yay up. Areepan would help her onboard. The sunlight was not so intense in the morning. Khun Yay was first peddled towards the east side of the temple. Then she would continue to the back of the temple where it was shadier. The attendant who rode Khun Yay's tri-shaw usually went at a moderate speed.

On her route, Khun Yay's tri-shaw passed by the Tāvatiṃsa building and headed toward the concrete bridge and the bell tower[1] and passed another bridge before reaching the *Pterocarpus* Rise.[2] The garden was shady and dense with *Pterocarpus* trees. Khun Yay always found many weeds in the area. She would ask the attendant to stop the tri-shaw so she could pull up weeds. As she became older, Khun Yay could not pull weeds herself. She simply watched her attendant working on the weeds from the seat of the tri-shaw. Her diligence unaffected by her age, even dressed in all her warm clothes, Khun Yay still couldn't resist pausing to do weeding or to dig up a sapling for replanting. She'd come asking for a

---

1. presently removed 2. *nern pradoo*

plastic bag from the kitchens saying:

"Small saplings are healthy ones. If they're just left there, the chickens will peck out the buds. It's better that I take them for replanting. Our temple could still do with planting a lot more trees."

Leaving the *Pterocarpus* Rise, she headed towards the temple's gleaming front gate, which was made from maintenance-free stainless steel. The gate had simple classic lines. The gate's shiny surface glinted in the warm morning sunlight. Khun Yay had complained that the previous gate had become old and rusty, so the attendant raised funds for a new stainless steel one. Seeing that the temple's wall had been made strong enough to last a thousand years the new gate should be good enough to last just as long.

As Khun Yay passed by different places in the temple, she would often recall the names of contributors who donated for the temple with thankfulness. From the front to the back of the temple, Khun Yay could remember the name of every contributor who had donated a building or facility.

From the temple's gate, the tri-shaw turned back toward the marble (then) reception building and Cātumahārājika Assembly Hall where workers would gather for chanting. A supervising monk attended the chanting, checking names of workers who joined the activity and supervising those sweeping and mopping. Some workers would greet Khun Yay by putting their her hands in a gesture of prayer. Khun Yay would return the workers' greeting and often she stopped to give them advice and guidance. Khun Yay mostly advised them how to keep the temple property clean and tidy. She taught them how to sweep fallen leaves properly and made sure they knew that the temple's tools were returned to their proper place after use.

Khun Yay made a point of teaching virtue not only to the congregation, but even to the labourers working at the temple itself. She didn't look upon the labourers as beneath learning about virtue. She didn't see them as merely labour hired to work day by day – but she wanted to learn as much about virtue as the opportunity allowed, so that this would be merit for them to take with them to lifetimes to come. It was for this reason that the labourers at the Dhammakāya Temple had an enormous respect for Khun Yay – as illustrated by the following conversation:

"My dear girl! What are you thinking about when you're planting that tree?"

"I wish that the tree won't die so that the vice-abbot won't get angry with us." Khun Yay asked someone else the same question and got the reply, "I wish that the tree would grow as quickly as possible so that we don't have to replant."

"And how about you?" she asked, turning to a third.

"I wish it won't die, but grow up fast so that passers-by can rest in its shade."

A fourth answered her, "I wish that anyone who sits at the foot of the tree I have planted will meditate well enough to see the Buddha inside clearly and without delay."

"Err! That's the sort of wish you ought to be making! You might expend just as much energy and get paid just the same wages as the next man for planting a tree, but you get more merit than the next!"

What Khun Yay taught the labourers on that occasion is pertinent to all pursuers of perfection with the moral that no matter what one may do, one's mind must remain in a wholesome state, avoiding the unwholesome.

Khun Yay would greet everyone in such a way even including the security guards around the temple. Sometimes, she asked "Do we have snacks for them?"

Anywhere else in the world, mere labourers wouldn't get much attention from their employees. If she didn't attend to them personally, she spoke to their supervisor such as Ven. Jhānabhiñño of the Construction and Maintenance Department, because the workers were seen as part of the temple community too.

Next, the tri-shaw brought Khun Yay to the monks' residential area where outsiders were normally forbidden to enter. Inside the area, there were about twenty small *kuti*s. These *kuti*s were strongly built — each of them designated to accommodate a single teaching monk. Mostly, only senior monks who were the temple's pioneers lived in this area. Each *kuti* is connected to the roadway by a small walkway. From the monks' *kuti*s, she continued to the meditation research workshop.[1] Following the route, she returned to the temple's office building 'Purohita'.

Khun Yay was at her best when she was on the tri-shaw inspecting the temple. As the temple's founder, everything that she saw in the temple reminded her of the great dedication and exceptional effort that she devoted to elevate everyone's life towards the Dhamma. When Khun Yay saw something messy she had to spend extra time and energy working on it. She

---

1. *akarn bhavana*

132

would train others to take care of the issue. She was still proud that she had tried her best to take care of the temple's property, the Lord Buddha's legacy, so that the new generation could continue to use them for the benefit of all. She used to say:

> "Whatever we have done, we have to follow up and take care of it. It is necessary to have a caretaker. I started this temple. I still have to follow up and take good care of it. I did everything. In the future, when the abbot and me are gone, all the future generations have to do is keep on looking after the place."

It took about an hour for her to complete her round. She usually arrived back at the office around nine o'clock. Sometimes inspecting *Purohita* would take longer than expected. Khun Yay would examine the building inside *and* out. Sometimes she would pause to talk to monks and laypeople. Khun Yay frequently visited this office building, especially when she found something wrong in the temple. She would inform the staff there of any problem she discovered so they could do something about it.

From *Purohita*, she returned to her *kuti* around nine o'clock. It was late in the morning, but the environment around the road way was still fresh and enjoyable.

At the old Public Relations building, she talked to Ven. Suvijjābho, who took care of the building, about how she handled all the messy spots within the temple:

> "Venerable Sir! You know, I still have to deal with those who cause all the mess. Do you know when the other people retire from their jobs? I'm eighty

133

three already, but I still have to continue,"

Khun Yay admitted things openly while talking to her student monk.

In addition to making her rounds of the temple, another favourite activity of Khun Yay was to examine the kitchen and surrounding areas, within walking distance. Khun Yay had special concern in the kitchen since she believed that an army marched on its stomach. Khun Yay frequently made the wish about the kitchen

> "May my meritorious deeds help me to be able to feed all the staff, no matter how many they are. May I have the means to support them. If there are a hundred, may I be able to feed a hundred. If there are a million, may I be able to feed a million."

It was common that Khun Yay visited the kitchen once or twice each day — for the simple reason that the abbot asked her to look after it. No matter what the abbot asked of her Khun Yay would do it to the best of her ability.

Khun Yay was a living example of perfection both in the subtle task of meditation and in the coarse work of temple upkeep and catering. She was the force majeure in the kitchens making sure the plates and cutlery were properly stored. She taught everyone to line up the crockery in neat lines on the draining board in a way that never failed to impress newcomers to the temple.

Arriving at the kitchen, Khun Yay surveyed the area on foot and taught:

> "All utensils must be properly arranged. Only if we have mastered virtues ourselves, will we be able to teach them to others. If we do everything

134

neatly and orderly, we will come across only neat and orderly things in the next lifetime."

Kitchenware was scrupulously sorted and organized, no matter what it was. Monks' and laypeoples' crockery were kept separately.

Khun Yay's eyesight was sharp and quick. With a single look, she could detect even tiny spots of dirt and untidiness. Ordinary people had to look at something several times to see as much as Khun Yay discovered with a single glance.

At Yāmā kitchen, utensils were kept in waist-high stainless steel cabinets. They lined both inside and outside the dining hall. Khun Yay explained:

"Before, we used open wood shelves, but a stray dog came along and relieved itself over the utensils. That's why I had the laypeople replace them with stainless steel cabinets."

Since there were so many cabinets, sometimes one or more of the doors were not properly closed. Khun Yay always inspected the cabinets to see if there were any doors left open. She warned the kitchen staff about the cabinets:

"If you leave the doors ajar, they will end up being snapped off at the hinges. Make sure all the cabinet doors are properly closed — otherwise pests will make their nests inside. We will end up using soiled utensils for our food. Be careful when you open and close the doors — make sure they are firmly closed."

Khun Yay added that slamming the cabinet doors and drawers would cause them to wear out before their time. If she found scratches on a stainless steel cabinet, she would summon all the staff in the kitchen to bear witness, telling them to be more cautious and prevent such damage in the future. Metal objects should not be allowed to scuff the cabinet's work surface — they should be lifted rather than slid. A protective piece of cloth should be laid beneath a chopping board before use. Food should be prepared elsewhere – not on top of the cabinets.

Khun Yay was like a living example of how to use and care for temple property. She always said:

"Spending your money wastefully, you become a slave to the money. Using electricity wastefully, you become slave to the electricity. Using water wastefully, you become slave to the water."

Khun Yay overlooked nothing. She tried her best to safeguard all the temple's property in keeping with the Buddha's teaching for ensuring the continued prosperity of any clan[1] that one should: look for lost possessions, mend broken possessions, know moderation in expenditure and not put unscrupulous people in charge of resources.

Khun Yay maintained mindfulness and caution when using the resources, no matter what they were. In addition to demonstrating know-how, she continued teaching the others around her without weariness.

When monks finished their meals, it was considered auspicious for the laypeople to finish the remainder themselves. The monks' utensils were cleaned and dried separately from those of the laypeople. To dry utensils, they were placed in an orderly fashion on <u>draining boards</u> made of stainless steel. Everything

1. A.ii.249

was sorted neatly by type. Once dry, the utensils would immediately be put away in the cabinets.

Khun Yay spent a lot of time teaching her growing community without any sign of reluctance. But somehow she showed her worries toward the new generation as she said:

> "It is fortunate that I live so long. I'm not sure if the next generation will be able to keep it up when I am gone."

Besides emphasizing cleanliness, discipline and good maintenance of the temple's property, Khun Yay also warned about making unnecessary noise especially from a chatting or clumsiness. She would reprimand those who made excessive noise right away. Every time Khun Yay walked into the kitchen, all the kitchen staff would keep silence and concentrate on their duties. They became more cautious and mindful while working. They improved themselves in many ways.

The front[1] and back kitchens[2] were separated. A big sliding stainless steel gate divided them. Near the gate, there was a location in the front kitchen where ingredients and raw materials such as onions, garlic, vegetables and fruit were stored. If Khun Yay saw that any of these raw materials had fallen on the floor, she would have them picked up immediately before they were wasted. She explained:

> "We must be cautious when using or spending the requisites donated out of faith. Do not use them carelessly because contributors made a wish

---

1. The front kitchen 'Yāmā' was used for small-scale preparation of meals for the teaching monks until 2003.
2. The back kitchen was used for large-scale production of food for the thousand-strong community and congregation.

upon the gifts they have donated. Otherwise, we will be in debt to them in future lifetimes."

A temple can only exist because of donations. Every penny counts. Contributors had worked their fingers to the bone in order to earn funds to donate to the temple – all out of the wish that the donation earn merit to improve their lot in life. They made their wishes over and over expecting that the temple would spend it in a way that would bring the maximum benefit. This is why temple staff needed to be especially responsible with requisites given out of faith.

Khun Yay was often to be seen in front of Yāmā dining room sitting teaching groups of laymen at her feet. Generally, there were three types of visitors who came to see Khun Yay. The first group was those who came to ask for spiritual help. The second group were those who came to thank Khun Yay for helping them successfully. The third were followers who visited her regularly. These latter came with offerings or simply came to greet Khun Yay. Many of these followers just loved to sit in the room listening to her giving guidance to others.

Generally, Khun Yay met her visitors every Sunday afternoon at Yāmā building and sometimes at lunchtimes on regular days too. Visitors would meditate with her in Tusitā Assembly Hall before the fish release ceremony on every third Saturday of the month. Visitors were from every walk of life and ranged from parents with toddlers to the aged in wheelchairs. Khun Yay could find a way of fitting in with all of them. Khun Yay welcomed everyone and talked to them with kindness regardless of their social status, gender or age. Her spiritual guidance was

simple and full of good wishes. Her words correspond-
ed to what her visitors sought or thought of, as if she
could read their minds. Khun Yay advised everyone
to be meritorious and refrain from demerit:

> "To be born as a human being is already fortu-
> nate. You all should learn how to make merit
> and be generous. After death, we take nothing
> with us but our merit and unwholesome deeds.
> If you make merit, you carry the merit with you.
> If you make demerit, you carry the demerit with
> you. It does not simply disappear after death.
> We continue to carry our merit and demerit."

Often, when some new visitors came to her, Khun
Yay said:

> "It's good that you come to the temple now. If
> you do not come here now, you will eventually
> be carried into the temple feet-first.[1]"

Khun Yay had special compassion for children, she
caressed them gently with her hands. Sometimes she
invited the parents to let her adopt their children — to
be their 'godparent'. Khun Yay said, "Some children
have a lot of merit from their previous lifetimes. Parents may find it difficult to give them sufficient spiritual support. I offer to take some of the responsibility
for childrens' spiritual upbringing." Some children
cried when they heard Khun Yay had adopted them.
Khun Yay would smile with kindness and add "I adopt
you only in name, but your parents will continue to
raise you as usual."

When young men came to see her, Khun Yay asked
"Have you ever been ordained?" If they hadn't

---

1. Most Thai people have their funeral ceremony at a Buddhist temple.

she'd advise, "As a man, you should have experience of ordination. Otherwise, you remain immature. You should be ordained and stay the duration of the Buddhist Lent before disrobing."

Some visitors came with photos of their deceased parents, siblings or relatives. They asked Khun Yay to help their beloved ones in the spiritual world. There was a young man who brought a very old photo of his father saying "Khun Yay! I would like you to find out where my late father is now. He passed away when I was young. I worry how he is these days." He handed over the father's photo to Khun Yay with the name and other details and requested to have the photo back afterwards. A week later, he came to see her again and asked for the photo. Areepan passed the photo to Khun Yay. Upon receiving it, Khun Yay looked at the photo again saying that she had already helped.

One day, there was a visitor who came with a title deed to a plot of land. She told Khun Yay after placing it on Khun Yay's desk, "I am having financial problems right now. I would like you to help by making a wish that someone buys this land. If I could sell it, I will pay off my debt and make a donation." Khun Yay simply replied "I will help." Later on, she came back with a donation in an envelope. Written on the front of the envelope were the words, "*I came to ask you for help in selling my land. Now that I have been able to sell it, my family members and I would like to express our utmost appreciation and gratitude. We also make donation in the amount of . . . for the Kaṭhina ceremony. Respectfully yours…*"

From word of the mouth, many more people visited

Khun Yay with their title deeds. Khun Yay was willing to help them all and there were many stories of miracles surrounding her. Many people came to her with worries — or if they were experiencing suffering. A lady came to Khun Yay with a picture, lamenting, "my mother is in the final stages of cancer." Khun Yay looked at the picture and whispered:

"It is difficult to recover from cancer. Tell your mother to pray, chant and be generous, so that she earns merit within. If she can not chant herself, you can chant for her while she is listening."

Finally, Khun Yay added:

"If it is impossible to help her while she is alive, it is still possible to help her after her death."

Khun Yay said quite often that those who got cancer had less chance to survive and would put her hands in a gesture of prayer making the wish:

"May I and others be spared this disease. May it disappear from this world."

Some visitors came to her in a hurry, "Khun Yay! My mother will have heart surgery today. She is already aged and I am afraid that she will be at risk. I am here to ask you to save her through the power of merit." Khun Yay replied

"Let your mother think only of meritorious deeds. There are both physical and spiritual factors. The doctor can fix the physical factors. But, spiritually, your mother must think of the merit she has done in the past and I will also help."

Cheered, the lady left immediately to see her mother

in hospital.

Some people were cheated by their close friends or relatives. They came to ask Khun Yay for help and guidance. Khun Yay listened to their accounts and replied:

"You can believe them, but don't *trust* them."

Some of the visitors came with ailments. There was a middle aged lady who told Khun Yay "I have been suffering from back pain. I have been searching for a cure from various famous doctors for such a long time, but it has not helped. I finally came to see you and you stroked my back with your hands. When I got home, there was no more pain. Now I am here to ask you to help *again* by massaging my arms." Khun Yay laughed a little bit and told her that she did not know how to do massage. In front of many other visitors, she simply moved close to Khun Yay and turned her back while begging "Can't you just touch?" Khun Yay chuckled and squeezed the lady's shoulder softly while saying "Please get well!" The lady was so happy, she bowed to Khun Yay and left the room joyously.

Khun Yay had to meet with various types of visitors and talked to all of them with sincerity and kindness. Everyone left the room with hope and their morale boosted. Khun Yay taught them to think of only meritorious deeds and good things because they would bring about success to one's life. She usually blessed them "May you be fulfilled in your good wishes through the power of merit."

Khun Yay's eyes showed compassion and thankfulness even for tiny offerings made to her. Sometimes when people greeted her with their hands in a gesture of prayer, she just held their hands in hers, transferring loving-kindness and warmth. Her eyes reflected the compassion, sincerity and warmth within her mind touching everyone's heart. She was the kind of senior citizen that everyone wanted to be close to.

The hot herbal tea placed at Khun Yay's side was left to turn cold many times. Khun Yay had to continue giving guidance to her visitors although she was so tired — but she still kept doing her duty with a joyful smile. It was the duty of a leader to many people on the Dhamma path. She never showed any signs of fatigue and never left early.

Some visitors also came for audience with Khun Yay at weekdays. These people usually were the emergency cases. They came to wait either in the kitchen or the walkways. Khun Yay never ignored them, she was willing to help and give guidance. There was a young lady who rushed to see Khun Yay while she was crossing the road to the office. Khun Yay asked her gently "What's the matter?" "Would you have time for me? Could we talk at Tusitā Hall?" she asked with sorrowful eyes. Although not well herself, Khun Yay walked to Tusitā Hall to listen her. The young lady had problems with her family. She cried as she told her story. Khun Yay listened to her for a long time and told her:

> "It is hard to be born as a human. Our present life is affected by past karma — by what we have done to ourselves in past lives. Thus, you must be patient and keep doing good deeds. Please be patient. We don't live so long and we must all die."

The lady added that there used to be a Buddhist nun who told her that she used to be a monkey in her past life. Khun Yay replied quickly:

"It doesn't matter what we were in the past life. But now we are human we have to rush to collect merit. You should graduate and get a job to support yourself, so that you don't have to rely on the others. I myself cannot read a word, but I can build a temple to help the others. I kept going. Before I went to Wat Paknam, I started as a maid, working for the others. I had to sweep, mop the floor, iron clothes and do many other chores — but I never gave up. We need to endure, no matter what others say about us."

Khun Yay gave her a lot of encouragement to brighten up her life.

Khun Yay taught meditation at Tusitā Pavilion and led the fish release ceremony for the group every third Saturday of the month. She gave instruction for meditation in short, meaningful phrases. It took her fifteen to thirty minutes for each meditation session. After closing her eyes, Khun Yay always started by saying:

"Let's sit to meditate. I will help guide you all. Keep your attention on the meditation. Now think of the merit and good deeds that we have accumulated. Think of all the merit from the fish-release."

While meditating, Khun Yay would say:

"Simply repeat the words 'Sammā-Arahaṃ,' we earn merit from meditation. It is not easy to attain Dhammakāya because our minds wander all around the world. We have to bring our mind back to the centre of our bodies, two fingers' breadths above the navel. Don't think of anything at all. When our minds become still,

144

it will be bright within. Stop the thoughts. Keep the mind quiet and still. Keep visualizing the clear Buddha. Be diligent in meditating. We will attain it in the next lifetime if we do not attain it in this one. We will build up the familiarity. To attain *Dhamma*, we need to practice with perseverance."

And Khun Yay ended each session with:

"Finally, with all the merit from our meditation, make wishes for good fortune, good health, prosperity, protection when travelling, freedom from danger, that fools keep their distance and that you attain inner experience while meditating . . . Now, let's rest at that. I would like to rejoice in your merit. May all of you have a lot of merit and be fulfilled in the good things that you wish for, through the power of merit. Good luck to all of you!"

Then all the visitors responded "*Sadhu!*" aloud. If any of the visitors had fallen asleep in their meditation, Khun Yay would say:

"I avoid falling asleep when meditating. If I feel sleepy, I go and rinse my face with water. I come back to meditate when the sleepiness has gone. People who fall asleep while meditating cannot attain inner experience."

Khun Yay loved meditation practice and it was so important to her.

Khun Yay remained particularly strict about any courting or petting between couples that took place on the temple grounds. Once as she was inspecting the temple grounds with Luang Phaw Dattajeevo (at that time there were no laywomen resident at the temple) she saw a labourer teenage couple playfully throwing soil at one another. From soil, they started to tease each other with sticks. Khun Yay observed and mentioned to Luang Phaw Dattajeevo:

"Don't let couples play around like that otherwise there will be repercussions for the whole of the temple. From throwing soil, they have started teasing each other with sticks. From sticks, they will start to get fresh with their hands. From catching at each other with their hands, they will soon be all over one another. Next time you see that sort of behaviour fire both of them, otherwise before long you'll have adultery taking place on the temple grounds."

Wat Phra Dhammakāya was supposed to be a sanctuary for meditation. Meditation had to be built on a foundation of purity of body, speech and mind and an amenable environment. Once rumours of any adultery in the temple grounds started to spread, the minds of people coming to the temple would be perturbed. The harmony in the temple community would be irreparably damaged – and this was the main reason that Khun Yay was extremely strict in this respect.

Khun Yay's even had the lower branches of the trees in the temple trimmed so that there would be no hiding place for secret intimacies. Khun Yay was very strict on this issue. If ladies entered into the area or went to see a monk, if no gentleman escort were available, they were supposed to find a female companion to accompany them.

Khun Yay foresaw the disadvantage of having a

146

spouse as well as the advantage of celibacy. She always made the wish that she remain single and be reborn in a virtuous family of Right View. Khun Yay had been autodidactic in this matter since she was young. She always advocated the advantages of celibacy. Many of her supporters stayed single their whole life long, because she would say:

> "It's good not to marry. You are single like me. Being single, we are like unencumbered little birds that can fly anywhere. The married ones are busy, they have to feed and take care of their families."

Alternatively, she would simply chide the single women with the warning, "Don't make eyes at the men!" or "Did you make eyes at anyone? Male and female know each other via their eyes. Looking at each other, they short circuit via their eyes and that's when they get irrevocably intimate."

Wat Phra Dhammakāya Temple has so many rules and regulations among monks, male staff, female staff and laymen that support the practice of celibacy. No-one could enforce rules about men and women looking at one another — so each had to take responsibility for themselves. Eyesight is also a kind of communication since 'the eyes are the window of your mind.' A single glance can mean more than a thousand words. Khun Yay always advised her students to cherish celibacy.

At the end of the day, before she went to bed, Khun Yay did her 'homework'. Khun Yay's homework was to help those who had visited her and made requests. Areepan brought pictures and details of those who had asked Khun Yay's help. She would inspect the pictures and have those messages read in detail.

Khun Yay listened to the requests attentively from the first until the last. She would ask Areepan if she had any doubts regarding the information. Then, Khun Yay entered her meditation in silence to help people. She would ask for more detail while she was meditating. For those who were in trouble and came to Khun Yay to request help, Khun Yay would help them with impartiality, sincerity and determination. She did not discriminate between people. It did not matter if the person was a new visitor or a familiar disciple. Khun Yay would try her best to help them whether she knew them or not.

Khun Yay's voice would murmur as she lay on her bed in silence in the darkness, with her hands in a gesture of prayer at her forehead while making the wish, "For those who came to see me asking for help, may they be fulfilled through the grace of merit." After a pause, putting her hands again in a gesture of prayer she would say "May all of those who came to see me for help be fulfilled."

One morning in November 1987 as Luang Phaw Dhammajayo was taking his breakfast, Khun Yay came humbly to his presence with her hands in a gesture of prayer. She said, "Venerable Sir! I have been thinking about something for two or three years now. I'd like to lead a Kaṭhina Ceremony myself. I am eighty now and for all I know, this might be my last chance. Please let me lead the Kaṭhina ceremony!"

Seeing Khun Yay's intent and humility, Luang Phaw said, "Go ahead Yay with my blessing. I'm happy for you to lead the 1988 Kaṭhina Ceremony."

A few days later Khun Yay returned saying that she

didn't want to do it any more. She explained, "It's not right for me to do it . . . against the regulations. Normally it must be a person *outside* the temple who leads the Kaṭhina Ceremony." Until that time, indeed the leader of the Kaṭhina Ceremony had always been a lay-supporter coming from outside the temple.

"Really Yay! You are the *founder* of this temple. If you are the leader of this Kaṭhina Ceremony, everyone will be ecstatic. Go ahead and be the Kaṭhina leader. *Everyone* will be glad for you!" It was only then that Khun Yay responded with the word '*Sadhu!*'

From that time onwards, wherever Khun Yay went, she would encourage others to share in '*her*' Kaṭhina by giving donations. She had her lay attendants drive her to every province from the far North to the deep South in order to visit all her old friends. She encouraged everyone she met. Everyone wanted to share in her Kaṭhina offering because they knew her Dhamma attainments to be very subtle and that the merit of this Kaṭhina ceremony would certainly be very special. Now when out and about on her tri-shaw, she would stop everyone she passed and encouraged them to share in the Kaṭhina merit with her.

Khun Yay would work hard in encouraging others to share in the merit as the leading contributor. Her heart was with merit all the time. She asked everyone she met to join her merit. Once, she said to the monks at the temple: "Venerable Sirs! Please help tell the laymen. As human beings, we should practise generosity to the full. All of us will die and all we can take with us is the merit and demerit we do before we die. Please help me by telling the laymen."

Thus, the following year on 6 November 1988, Khun Yay led the Kaṭhina ceremony at the temple. That day the temple was packed to standing room only with congregation members who had come to wish her well. It was not the only time for Khun Yay, but she led the Kaṭhina many subsequent times and robe-offering ceremonies too. In total, Khun Yay was to go on to be the president of the Kaṭhina ceremony ten times and for the robe offering ceremony twenty times.

When in 1994 Luang Phaw Dhammajayo announced that he wanted to pay homage to the Great Abbot of Wat Paknam by casting his image in solid gold, Khun Yay exclaimed:

> *"Sadhu!* That I have tirelessly devoted myself to training up students of the Dhammakāya Tradition so that this temple can have been built over the last twenty years, even to the point of collapsing from exhaustion on occasion – has all been out of my homage to the Great Abbot of Wat Paknam. However, all of this homage had been something I have kept to myself. I have always wanted to make an overt token of my devotion. Thus I rejoice in the merit of your wanting to cast his image in solid gold. I will help to bring together all those with seasoned perfections to help in its completion."

Thus it came to pass that Luang Phaw Dhammajayo, Khun Yay and assembled disciples of the Great Abbot of Wat Paknam from throughout Thailand joined to express their homage to the Great Abbot by casting his image with an entire ton of solid gold on 25 February 1994 with H.E. Somdej Phra Mahā Rājamaṅgalacharn, the present abbot of Wat Paknam, presiding over the ceremony.

Shortly afterwards, when Luang Phaw Dhamma-jayo gave the opportunity to help in the building of the Mahā Dhammakāya Cetiya as the focus of faith for Buddhists all over the world, Khun Yay was excited at the prospect and gave her full support even though at that time her health was no longer as strong. Although Khun Yay had some feeling that this might be a great task and might delay Luang Phaw from researching the knowledge of Dhammakāya, she realized the importance of the project to the Buddhist ministry to the world.

At that time, the thousand-acre area of land where the Cetiya was to be built, was still an empty plot of land. The Dhamma grounds were only used for ceremonies such as Māgha Pūjā and almsgiving in the morning. At the time when the Dhamma grounds were being prepared for the construction of the Cetiya, the field was full of mountains of earth. There was a flagpole with a red flag marking the point that would be the centre of the cetiya when it was finished.

Khun Yay would inspect the site expectantly. As the heat of the sun diminished in the evening, once Khun Yay went and bowed in front of the big white Buddha image located in the field and wished:

> "Venerable Sir! Please help me raise funds for the robes offering ceremony. May we receive a lot of contributions to help construct the Cetiya. May I be healthy. I feel so weak now."

At the time when the foundation piles were being driven, Khun Yay often complained:

> "Digging over and over. When will they start building the Cetiya? I don't know if I shall see the completion of the Cetiya."

Then she continued:

> "May we receive a lot of contributions so that the Cetiya can be completed quickly. I had a lot of Buddha relics given to me by Khun Yay Thongsuk. I offered them to Ven. Dhammajayo along with many other people. He said he would place these relics in the Cetiya. I don't know when the construction will be completed. I don't know if I will survive and see its completion. May we receive a lot of contributions to complete the construction quickly."

On 22 April 2000 which was the first grand inauguration day of the Cetiya, Khun Yay witnessed the congregation of monks, novices and laypeople from every part of Thailand and abroad. The Dhamma field was full of the saffron colour of monks' robes and white colour of lay people's dress — although she no longer had the strength to walk anymore. Sometimes it seems that her concern about the completion of the structure was the thing that kept her going in her final years.

Generally speaking, Khun Yay was healthy for her age. She was energetic even when she was eighty-three years old. Her back was straight, her eyes and ears were alert. Her skin was also fresh. Khun Yay had virtually no signs of senile forgetfulness. Behind her healthy appearance, Khun Yay had minor illnesses, however, which were due to aging such as dizziness and frequent visits to the bathroom. Khun Yay also had muscular aches and stiffness. It was difficult for her to raise her arms and sit cross-legged or sideways.

Khun Yay frequently got dizziness. She said the

doctor explained to her that it was due to low blood volume. She needed herbal medicine when she got dizziness and to have her hands and feet massaged as she lay down. She also had traditional massage on some occasions.

Not so long afterwards it was necessary to look after Khun Yay's health more carefully. Her straight back started to bend and her legs got numb when she meditated. It was not as easy for her to sit cross-legged as in the past. She would warn the youngsters:

> "As young people, you don't know what it is like to be numb and have your waist ache. You will know when you get old. When I was young, I could meditate six hours at a time during the day and another six hours at night. As youngsters, do what you should do *now* because you may not be able to do it when you get old."

When older, Khun Yay simply changed her meditation posture from sitting cross-legged to lying down due to the old age of her physical body. However, her internal vision remained sharp despite the change of her posture.

Although it is inevitable for one's physical body to deteriorate, Khun Yay never let it obstruct her from purification of her mind. She might not be able to sit and meditate for a long time, but she could still meditate while lying down. "I cannot sit and meditate for a long time now. So, I lie down to meditate and think of meritorious deeds."

Due to her great patience, Khun Yay kept to her normal schedule and met with her visitors every

Sunday except in case of an emergency (which was rare). She always asked, "How long have the visitors had been waiting for me? I don't want them to be disappointed. At least, I should show up, so that they can see me."

Later on, after Khun Yay started to gain weight, she looked fresh and joyful all the time. Those around her would experience her warmth and smiles, however, her health was deteriorating.

Later on, as Khun Yay got older if she had dizzy spells, she had to cancel her daily inspection by tri-shaw. On the good days, she made the inspection as before saying, "I love to ride on the tri-shaw. It is not shaky like other vehicles." She liked the tri-shaw because it could take her anywhere she wanted, even to corners or areas inaccessible by road. As she got older, Khun Yay's tri-shaw was replaced by an electric caddy car, which could only navigate sizable roadways. She did not have opportunities to visit certain spots as in the past.

Khun Yay started to have dizziness when it rained. Since her *kuti* was surrounded by many trees, it was quite damp in her room. She moved temporarily to the Tāvatiṃsa building which used to be the work place of the audio section. There was a lot of studio equipment inside, but there was enough room to accommodate Khun Yay. She lived at Tāvatiṃsa building temporarily. During this time, the abbots did all in their power to help her including building this new *kuti* for her. She moved to the *Dhammabarn kuti* in 1990 — a place designed to get Khun Yay out of the damp environment of the temple's eighty-acre area. This new *kuti* for Khun Yay's was built on the 1000-acre plot of land between the *Pariyatti Dhamma* School and Meditation Village. The new *kuti* was built out of her disciples' wish to accommodate Khun Yay as well as possible during her final years.

The *Dhammabarn Kuti* was designed to accommodate Khun Yay during her old age by facilitating her daily life and activities. It comprised two single-storey concrete buildings connected by a sheltered walkway for exercise. The entrance had a ramp for wheelchair access. There is a parking space in front of the entrance. The *kuti* was surrounded by fence and a pond to maintain privacy. In front of the *kuti* was a pond with a flight of steps, so that Khun Yay could release or feed fish. There was a roadway all the way around the perimeter with gardens and a lawn around the *kuti* itself. The garden was filled with aromatic plants.

Dhammabarn Kuti was close to monks and novices from the *Pariyatti Dhamma* School. Groups of monks and novices regularly passed by Khun Yay's new *kuti*. Khun Yay could see them from her room or even give them alms.

In 1996, Khun Yay's exhaustion became more noticeable. Sometimes she looked as if she might pass out. She spent most of her time in the hospital during the year 1996-1997, especially from September to November 1997. She stayed overnight in hospital for physical check ups. Her visits to the hospital were not disclosed, so that she wouldn't be exhausted by visitors.

When Khun Yay got well and was brought back to *Dhammabarn kuti* at the temple, some people were surprised that she still said "I want to go home."[1]

Externally, Khun Yay looked to be healthy, fresh and cheerful — but her attendant Areepan had to appeal to her several times a day "Please be healthy and live until the celebration of the **Dhammakāya Cetiya**." After the first celebration of the **Dhammakāya Cetiya**, Areepan appealed to Khun Yay to be healthy and live until the third celebration of the Cetiya.

---

1. In fact she was referring to her return to the fourth level of heaven from whence she had come.

13
Her Demise & Funeral

"We're all already in our old-age. Don't go thinking you're still young. I've thought of myself as 'old' since my youth — to give myself a sense of urgency in the pursuit of Perfection.
(Khun Yay, 24 March 1981)

It had been a long time since Khun Yay had been in hospital. The previous time was 22 November 1997. Even this time when she was admitted to Kasemrat Hospital, Bangkok on 6 September 2000, everyone expected that Khun Yay would recover and be back at the temple before long.

However, on 9 September 2000 she was still in intensive care. She lay with her eyes closed — still looking good in spite of what the doctors said. Everyone hoped for some kind of miracle.

Her best white robes were fetched from the temple — the ones which she used only on the first Sunday of each month and for major festivals. A set of fine monk's robes was also brought together with Khun Yay's biggest crystal ball which was about ten centimetres in diameter — these latter were intended to be Khun Yay's gift to the monastic community. The gifts were passed to Khun Yay to make wishes prior to them being offered to the abbot as alms. No special emotion showed on Khun Yay's face.

That night Khun Yay was still stable, and a special bag was added to the gifts — a bag containing all the bank notes Khun Yay had collected from donations. Khun Yay told her attendant to have it offered to the abbot. Inside the bag were wads of light brown envelopes tied together. Each envelope contained bank notes which were neatly arranged. It had always been Khun Yay's habit to fold and smooth bank notes grouping the denominations together with rubber bands.

That was Khun Yay's last meritorious deed because at 3 a.m., she passed away peacefully, at the age of 92. At dawn of 10 September 2000, the room turned completely quiet — those present reflecting on her epitaph, "I have been overcoming adversity throughout my life. If we are alive, we have to move on. We rest when we die. If we backslide, we will be defeated by Māra."

In the evening, Ven. Dattajeevo, senior monks and Khun Tavorn came with a casket which had been made upon the abbot's command. It had been designed especially in homage to Khun Yay's meritorious deeds. Khun Yay's casket was carved of solid teak five centimetres in thickness. The external surface was completely pasted with gold leaf. The case was panelled on the inside with a three-centimetre layer of fragrant sandalwood. Khun Yay's body was dressed in her white robe — the symbol of celibacy. Her face showed a slight smile. The body was wound in forty-three layers of soft white fabric. The wrapped body was sprinkled all over with jasmine oil. During the whole process, chanting was done in praise of Khun Yay. Her body was placed in the wooden casket and sprinkled again with jasmine oil. The wooden casket was then closed and sealed. The wooden casket was then covered by a decorative casket made of solid silver and gold. Inside the golden casket were silver sheets woven together as a box. The exterior of the casket was made from real thin gold sheets woven together by a traditional goldsmith. Later on, Khun Yay's disciples joined together to offer a funeral shroud woven from solid gold threads called the '*Maha Suwanna Ratana Bhusa*' to Khun Yay. It was used to drape the golden casket. The edges of this golden fabric were decorated with different kinds of precious stones. The shroud was embroidered with the words "In memory of Mahā Ratana Upāsika Chandra Khon-nok-yoong" Everything was superlatively made with love and respect for Khun Yay who was a great teacher to her disciples. It was deserving for Khun Yay who had always had great gratitude for her own teachers.

Daily Abhidhamma funeral chanting was arranged from 17 September 2000 to 2 February 2001. Senior monks and executives of monastic orders from various temples throughout the country came to recite the Abhidhamma. There were a hundred monks each working day and two-hundred monks on Sundays with thousands of laypeople also in attendance.

Khun Yay's last rites were held on 3 February 2002 in accordance with her wish to be cremated.

Senior monks from 30,000 Buddhist temples all over Thailand, together with senior monks from twenty different countries all around the world — a total of 100,000 monks, were present in the final cremation ceremony before a hundred thousand laypeople, the biggest-ever assembly of monks known in Buddhist history.

14
Epilogue[1]

"Listen carefully to my words. To have been born human is the greatest of good fortune. No other form of birth excels human birth. Life passes us by so fast — days and nights soon become years. Life doesn't wait for us. Having achieved human birth, we have to cultivate wholesomeness, practise generosity and do good deeds. We cannot take anything away with us from this life except the wholesomeness and unwholesomeness we have accrued during our life. We should make sure we accrue nothing but wholesomeness so that this is all we take with us. In this way we will have the wealth to pursue perfection in every lifetime. Doing only wholesome deeds and shunning all unwholesomeness, nothing will accrue to us but the meritorious fruits of the good deeds we have done by our volition. We can suffer no retribution from evil we have never done. When we pass away, we leave behind the evils we've never done, but take the wholesome things we have done with us.

Pursuing perfection is no easy thing. You need to be patient and you need to overcome obstacles. I have struggled to the best of my ability throughout my life. Now I thank all of you and bid you farewell. May great merits accrue to all of you who have accompanied me on the spiritual path. We will

1. Message recorded by Khun Yay shortly before her passing and replayed at her cremation on 3 February 2002.

161

all meet again on the path.

May all of you be endowed with wealth in this life and every future lifetime. May you have sufficient wealth to cultivate generosity without end. May all of you attain crystal clear enlightenment inside, attain the *Dhammakāya* without delay. If ever you cannot think of a solution to your problems, make sure you meditate on the problem and you will find a solution. May all of you be happy forever. May you all have a long life of pursuing wholesomeness. May your every wish come true by virtue of the generosity all of you have cultivated. May all of us meet up again on the spiritual path in every future lifetime. But now it is time for me to part from all of you . . ."

Index

land for donations 140; ate out of duty 52; attains inner bodies 29; autodidactic 54; big hands 12; birth 12; birthday celebration 97; bravery 13; brightness of mind 39; brought up to be diligent 14; brought up to be honest 14; checks language of animals 39; cheerful disposition 13; cleanliness 95, 94, 8, 127; compassion 12, 142, 8, 13; connected between shifts 48; consideration for others 126; contented with little 53; daily routine in 1960's 73; death 158; decisive personality 71; definitive in decisions 119; demanding little 12; determination to reach Nirvana 8; did not let obstacles interfere with meditation 58; diligence 22; discipline 22, 8; discouraged marriage 112, 147; discourages blind trust of others 142; discourages chatting 137; discourages clumsiness 137; discourages unnecessary noise 137; disinterested in exterior trappings of wealth 51; dismisses fate from past lives 144; doubts calibre of future generations 137; durian incident 53; early hindrances in meditation 25, 28; early riser 11; earnest meditator 26; economized on tap water 126; emaciated appearance 42; encouraged celibacy 96, 147; encouraged Phrarajbhavanavisudh 89; encouraged patience in the face of difficulty 143; encouraged young men to ordain 140; encourages education 98; encourages unity 111; endurance 14; exhaustion 155; faith heals back pain 142; favours maintenance free

amenities 130; fifth born daughter 12; first meeting with Phrarajbhavanavisudh 85; first meeting with Phramongkolthepmuni 37; first news of Phramongkolthepmuni 18; first to greet guests 119; fledglings of 8; fond of trees 108; fond of trees 109; forms team of successors 94; fund raising 151, 150, 149, 110; funeral message 161, 162; funeral rites 159; gifts crystal ball to monastic community 157; gratitude 126, 130, 142, 68, 8, 13; guardian of the rare crystal balls 54; happiness of attainment 29; head of late shift 48; healthy until close to death 152; helped sick 78; homework 147; humility towards youngest monks 119; ill from undernourishment 109; illiterate 9; impatient that Dhammakaya Cetiya should be completed 151; impulsive 13; in war effort 84; inner virtue 8; instructed to perpetuate Dhammakaya tradition 64; instructs meditation 144; instructs meditation 145; kept fields clear of weeds 11; kept mind at centre constantly 43, 56; kitchen hygiene 95; lack of education 14; lay down to meditate when old 153; lays temple rules 116, 117, 118; leads cleaning of the toilets 121; leads Kathina ceremony 148; *kuti* (nimanarati) 125, 126; learned without reading 46; leaves home 19-20; liked orderliness 127; little skill in public speaking 71; lively 13; looked up afterlife destinations 140, 54; love of children 139; loved pets 13; loved swim-

166

Khon-nok-yoong 26

earnings, Chandra Khon-nok-yoong presented all to mother 14

eating: out of duty, Chandra Khon-nok-yoong 52; monks' leftovers 136

economic values, Buddhist 103

economical toilet flushing 122

education, Chandra Khon-nok-yoong's lack of 14; encouraged by Chandra Khon-nok-yoong 98

Eight Precepts 103

Eighteen Elements 46

electioneering prohibited in temple 118

electricity, saving 136

Elements, Eighteen 46

elusiveness of inner experience 27

emaciation of Chandra Khon-nok-yoong 42

embers criticism, Chandra Khon-nok-yoong afraid of 49

endurance of Chandra Khon-nok-yoong 14

enlargement of Wat Paknam predicted 63

environment hinders meditation if messy 128

establishment of Dhamma Practice Centre 102; temple kitchen 117; Wat Phra Dhammakaya 104

Eucalyptus trees 108

exaggerated gestures prohibited in temple 118

exemplars: Phrarajbhavanavisudh 92; Chandra Khon-nok-yoong 121

exhaustion of Chandra Khon-nok-yoong 155

expansion of Dhammaprasit group 91; of Wat Phra Dhammakaya 124

expenditure, moderation in 136

experience, inner 26

exploration of heaven 49

eyes of Chandra Khon-nok-yoong sincere 12

Faculties, Twenty-two 46

faith healing by Chandra Khon-nok-yoong 142

fame of Chandra Khon-nok-yoong prophesised 79

family life, discouraged 44, 94

fate from past lives dismissed by Chandra Khon-nok-yoong 144

father of Chandra Khon-nok-yoong 12

Ferry, Chao Phraya River 86

field of merit, pure monks 43

final words of Phramongkolthep-muni 66

finances for Wat Phra Dhammakaya 106, of Chandra Khon-nok-yoong's family 14

fish release ceremony 144; unanswerable question about salted 51

Five Aggregates 45

Five Precepts 33

fledglings of Chandra Khon-nok-yoong 8

floor of toilet, kept dry 122

flowery words, rarely used by Chandra Khon-nok-yoong 71

flushing toilets economically 122

food that had been dropped, should be picked up 137; Chandra Khon-nok-yoong wished to provide sufficient of all-comers 134

forgiveness sought from dying relatives 17; Chandra Khon-nok-yoong asks for father's 35

fortune-telling prohibited in temple 118

169

176

Bibliography

Heikkilä-Horn, Marja-Leena (1996) "Two paths to Revivalism in Thai Buddhism: The Dhammakaya and Santi Asoke Movements", *Temenos* 32, pp.93-111.

McDaniel, Justin (2006) "Modern Buddhism in Thailand" in *Buddhism in World Cultures: Comparative Perspectives* ed. Steven Berkwitz, Santa Barbara, CA: Oxford ABC Clio pp.101-128.

na Songkhla, Natayada (1999) *Style and Ascetics: Attractiveness, Power and the Thai Sangha*, unpublished PhD Dissertation: SOAS, University of London.

How to Meditate

Meditation is a state of ease, inner peace and happiness that we can bring into being, ourselves. It is a practice recommended by Buddhism for happiness, non-recklessness, mindfulness and wisdom in everyday life. It is no mystery, but something which can be easily practised by all following the technique taught by Phramonkolthepmuni (Sodh Candasaro), Luang Phaw Wat Paknam as follows:

Step-by-Step Instructions for the Meditation Technique

(1) Paying respect to the Triple Gem: To start one should soften one's mind by paying respect to the Triple Gem, before taking Five or Eight Precepts to consolidate one's virtue;

(2) Recollect your goodness: Kneel or sit with your feet to one side and think of all the good deeds you have done throughout the day, from your past, and all the good deeds you intend to do in the future. Recollect such good deeds in such a way, until you feel as if your whole body seems to be filled with tiny particles of goodness;

(3) Sit for meditation, relaxing body and mind: Sit in the half-lotus position, upright with your back and spine straight - cross-legged with your right leg over the left one. Your hands should rest palms-up on your lap, and the tip of your right index finger should touch your left thumb. Try to find a position of poise for yourself. Don't take up a position where you have to force or stress yourself unnaturally - but at the same time, don't slouch! Softly close your eyes as if you were falling asleep. Don't squeeze your eyes shut and make sure you have no tension across your eyebrows. Relax every part

of your body, beginning with the muscles of your face, then relax your face, neck shoulders, arms, chest, trunk and legs. Make sure there are no signs of tension on your forehead or across your shoulders. Focus on the task in hand, creating a feeling of ease in your mind. Feel that the you are entering upon a supreme state of calm and ease with both body and mind.

(4) Imagine a crystal ball as the object of your meditation: Imagine a clear, bright, flawless crystal ball as if it is floating at the centre of your body (*see seventh base of the mind in the illustration*). The crystal ball should be pure and soothing, like twinkling starlight to the eye. At the same time, softly repeat the sound of the mantra '*Sammā-Arahaṃ*' to yourself as 'recollection of the Buddha' over and over again. Alternatively you can start by imagining the crystal ball at the first base of the mind, and gradually move it down to the seventh base via the other six bases (*see diagram*) while repeating the mantra to yourself.

*

Once the crystal ball becomes visible at the centre of the body, continue to maintain a feeling of ease, as if the mental object seen is part of that feeling. If the crystal ball should disappear, don't feel disappointed - just keep the same feeling of ease in your mind as before, and imagine a new crystal ball in place of the old. If the mental object should appear anywhere else other than the centre of the body, gradually lead the object to the centre of the body, without using even the slightest of force. When the mental object has come to a standstill at the centre of the body, place the attention at the centre of that object, by imagining that there is an additional tiny star visible there. Focus your mind continuously on the tiny star at the centre of the object of meditation. The

THE SEVEN BASES
OF THE MIND

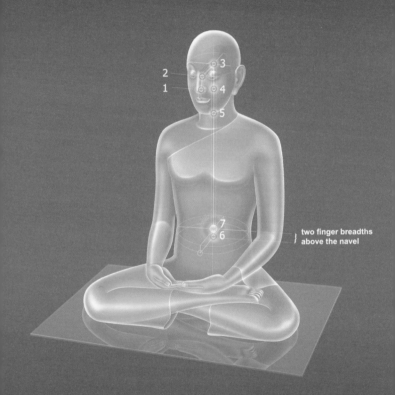

two finger breadths
above the navel

mind will adjust itself until it comes to a perfect stand-still. At that point, the mind will fall through the centre and there will be a new brighter sphere which arises in place of the original one. This new sphere is known as the 'Pa.thama-magga sphere' or 'sphere of Dhamma'. This sphere is the gateway or trailhead to the pathway to Nirvana.

Imagining the object of meditation is something you can do the whole of the time, wherever you may be, whether sitting, standing, walking, lying-down or performing other activities.

It is advised to imagine in such a way continuously at every moment of the day - but imagining without force. No matter how well you manage, you should be contented with your level of progress, in order to prevent excessive craving for immediate results becoming a hindrance to your progress. If you meditate until having attained a steadfast, diamond-bright 'sphere of Dhamma' at the centre of your body, you should try to maintain it by recollecting it as continuously as you can.

In such a way, the benefits of your meditation will not only keep your life on the pathway of happiness, success and non-recklessness, but also ensure your continuing progress in meditation.

ADDITIONAL ADVICE

1. *Avoid force:* Never force anything in your meditation. Don't squeeze your eyes closed thinking you will see the object of meditation more quickly. Don't tense your arms, your abdomen or your body - because any form of tension will only cause the mind to be displaced from the centre of the body to the place you are tensing.

2. **Don't crave after seeing something:** You should al-

ways maintain complete neutrality of mind. Don't let your mind be distracted from the object of meditation and the mantra. Don't worry yourself about when the object of meditation will appear. The image will appear itself when it comes to the right time, just as the sun rises and sets in its own time.

3. ***Don't worry about your breath:*** Meditating in this technique starts with the visualization of a bright object [*āloka kasiṇa*]. Once having meditated until attaining the sphere of Dhamma, one continues with meditation by passing through the refined human body (astral body), the angelic body, the form-Brahma body and the formless-Brahma body until attaining the Dhamma body (or *Dhammakāya*). Only then is one equipped to turn one's meditation towards insight [*vipassanā*]. Thus there is no need to practise mindfulness of the breath at any stage.

4. ***Maintain your mind at the centre of the body all the time:*** Even after having finished your formal sitting, maintain your mind at the centre of the body the whole of the time. No matter whether you are standing, walking, sitting or lying-down, don't allow your mind to slip away from the centre of the body. Continue repeating the mantra '*Sammā-Arahaṃ*' to yourself while visualizing the crystal ball at the centre of the body.

5. ***Bring all objects arising in the mind to the centre of the body:*** No matter what appears in the mind, bring it (gently) to the centre of the body. If the object disappears, there is no need to chase around looking for it. Just continue to rest your attention at the centre of the body while repeating the mantra to yourself. Eventually, when the mind becomes yet more peaceful, a new object of meditation will appear.

The basic meditation described here will lead to a deepening of happiness in life. If one doesn't abandon the practice but cultivates meditation regularly, to the point that the sphere of Dhamma is attained, one should try to maintain that sphere at the centre of one's body for the remainder of one's life, while leading one's life in a scrupulous way. It will offer one a refuge in life and will bring happiness both in this lifetime and the hereafter.

SUMMARY OF THE BENEFITS OF MEDITATION
1. Personal Benefits for the meditator
- *The Mind:* the mind will feel at ease - calm and peaceful. Memory will also improve;
- *Personality:* self-confidence will be improved. The true nature of calm will become apparent. Anger will diminish, leaving only the feeling of kindness towards others;
- *Daily life:* will be increased in quality in the new-found absence of stress. The results of work or study will be much more successful. The meditator can enjoy health of both body and mind;
- *Ethics and decision-making:* a right understanding of that which is good and that which is bad, will be clearly seen for any given situation. Important decisions will cause less worry because the meditator understands the outcome of his actions. The meditator can refrain from harmful actions and decisions, instead being content and confident about choices made.

2. Benefits for the Meditator's Family
- *Peace and success:* family life will be more harmonious, through the increased mutual respect and consideration between family members. Parents will be better able to lead the family successfully;

- *Cooperation:* Family members will be more enthusiastic to honour their duties and co-operate towards solving shared problems.

3. **National Benefits**

- *Peaceful Society:* most grave social problems originate from unwholesomeness of mind. If everybody learns to meditate and live peacefully, 'endemic' problems like crime and drug abuse will be diminished;

- *Respect:* Respect for others will be improved simply through keeping to a routine of meditation and following moral precepts. Honesty will diminish suspicion in the community;

- *A caring society:* as a result of meditation, the peacefulness of life can be more widely enjoyed and there will be a more widespread willingness to participate in social work

4. **Spiritual Benefits**

- *Understanding eternity:* all people, with or without their own faith can deepen the understanding of their own spirituality through meditation. Meditators of all faiths, through the practice of meditation, can explore their own faith in depth, particularly with reference to the understanding of eternity in their chosen faith;

- *Inspiration:* inspiration in your own spiritual tradition is strengthened as the meditator comes to realize the profound happiness that can be found through meditation;

- *Prolonging the lifetime of spiritual traditions:* the meditator's own spiritual tradition will be maintained as newcomers have a better understanding of moral conduct and self-discipline.

Acknowledgments

This book draws on the biography of Khun Yay from three different Thai sources. The relevant chapters of *Deun bai su kwam suk* (c.1970) compiled by various authors was translated by Chalermsri Pongsai. Prapasri Boonsuk's 1998 biography of Khun Yay was translated by Phra Nicholas Thanissaro. Ratanamala's (2002) biography of Khun Yay's final years *Yoo kap Yay* was translated by Pittaya Tisuthiwong and sub-edited by Mark David George. The three sources were compiled and re-edited into a single book by Phra Nicholas Thanissaro. For the first edition, additional thanks are deserved by Chatchai Sribundith, Puengpit Poopornanake, Wallop Niltanom, Preecha Ounrasameewong, Buddhist Graphic Arts Department of the Dhammakāya Foundation, Oranuj Thitiyanaporn and Chalom Srijarus for design and administrative assistance. For the second edition, thanks are due for corrections submitted by Dr. Chanida Jantrasrisalai and administrative assistance rendered by Phra Ronnaphob Jotilabho and Panpimon Pantamit.

Follow-up Contacts

International Branches: There are more than fifty Dhammakaya meditation centres worldwide which offer a selection of activities on Buddhism and meditation in Thai and local languages. An up-to-date list of contacts can be found at:

www.dhammakaya.net/en/centers/center-continent

World Peace Ethics Contest: A multi-lingual yearly contest to test knowledge of Buddhist ethics as they relate to the family is organized at Dhammakaya branches worldwide:

www.vir2kidz.com

Dhammakaya Meditation Retreats: Meditation retreats following the Dhammakaya Tradition can be booked with the Middle Way meditation retreats in Thailand and on tour abroad:

www.meditationthai.org

Temporary Ordination: An international ordination scheme is held each July at the main Dhammakaya Temple in Thailand in English and Mandarin:

www.ordinationthai.org

Distance Learning: By distance learning it is possible to study Buddhism and meditation at degree level via Dhammakaya's Open University:

www.dou.us

Peace Revolution: meditation mentoring and activities in Thailand for an online community of young people in non-religious context can be found at:

www.peacerevolution2010.org

Khun Yay Maharatana Upasika Chandra Khon-nok-yoong (1909-2000).
Leading disciple of the Great Abbot of Wat Paknam Bhasicharoen and
founder of Wat Phra Dhammakaya.

(above) Khun Yay allowed her leading student to be ordained 'Dhammajayo Bhikkhu' at a ceremony held on 27 August 1969 at Wat Paknam Bhasicharoen (below) Khun Yay perpetuated the Dhammakaya tradition through the sixties until overcrowding of Dhammaprasit House necessitated expansion at a new site in Pathum Thani province called 'Wat Phra Dhammakaya' in 1970.

(above) Lady Prayat Paetyapongsavisudhathibodee offers eighty-acres of land in Pathum Thani province with ground breaking on 20 February 1970 for the establishment of the 'Dhamma Practice Centre' (below) Bird's eye view of the eighty-acre site c.1977 after the canals had been dredged, the majority of the trees planted and the main chapel in mid-construction.

Khun Yay aged around eighty, pictured behind the main chapel.

(above) The students' 'Dhammadayada' ordination which has been taking place at the temple annually since 1972 (below) the 29-metre peak of the Khun Yay memorial vihara [enshrining a golden statue of Khun Yay] which with its votive beacon, was completed in September 2003.

(above) Khun Yay with some of the peacocks and chickens inhabiting the sanctuary wooded by trees she grew by her own hand (below) Khun Yay making her daily inspection of the temple by trishaw.

(above) Khun Yay encouraging a congregation to share in her first Kathina offering of 1988 (below) Khun Yay attends the World Meditation Day ceremony held at Wat Phra Dhammakaya with tens of thousands of others.

Khun Yay was president of the Kathina ceremony at Wat Phra Dhammakaya on 6 November 1988 and ten subsequent times.